forgotten TALES of MICHIGAN'S LOWER PENINSULA

Alan Naldrett

illustrations by
Cait Brennan

London

Published by The History Press
Charleston, SC 29403
www.historypress.net

First published 2014

Manufactured in the United States

ISBN 978.1.62619.658.2

Library of Congress CIP data applied for.

This book is dedicated to Lynn Keck Lyon, who accompanied me on research trips to Toledo, Monroe, Detroit and environs and has learned to really like the Nain Rouge, Toledo War and the King of Beaver Island, at least as much as anyone can actually like them.

PREFACE

In chronicling the not-so-well-remembered tales of Michigan, doing it chronologically seemed logical. This means starting with such lore as the Nain Rouge and the Snake Goddess of Belle Isle, in which is mentioned the destruction of a Native American stone idol on Belle Isle (which is probably mostly true, including the document left at the scene with the cross). However, the ending of the tale should be easily recognized as legend, unless one is used to seeing pieces of stone idols turn into snakes.

In the latter part of the book, when I am describing events that have more historical evidence, such as the Toledo War, I have been as factual as possible. However, when I set out to write the story of the Toledo War, the first thing I noticed was the serious demeanor with which historians treated it. No wonder most people don't remember it! You would think that people would at least recall the account about the Michigan and Ohio armies that never engaged in battle because both got lost in the Great Black Swamp. Maybe the reason this event is not well recorded in the history books is because both sides were too embarrassed to admit to it to provide more detailed information.

Another event in the Toledo War was about a court session that Ohio held at three o'clock in the morning to cement Ohio's claim to Toledo. Unfortunately, the notes that would prove the court session ever took place were lost while their keepers were running from a phantom Michigan militia. This is, again, probably one of those stories that people didn't like to brag about, although these facts have been documented with the same reverence given a war with actual battles and fatalities.

A big problem with the historic accounts of the Toledo War is that it was probably still "too early" for people to see the humor in the fact that the only injury was the stabbing of a deputy sheriff with a knife smaller than a jackknife, causing minimal damage. (In all fairness, there were a few other injuries—a few pigs were confiscated and roasted.)

Another point worth mentioning is the difference in sense of humor over the years. The historian of one hundred years ago would note "humorous" incidents and then relate a story such as the Michiganders saying, "Here's to Major Stickney's potatoes and onions—we drafted their tops and their bottoms volunteered" while stealing vegetables. This knee-slapper has also been rendered as "drafting his [Stickney's] potato vines to make volunteers of the bottoms." Most people would agree that this illustrates a definite difference in the quality of humor in the Michigan Territory in the 1800s compared to that of modern day. Also, I have read many accounts of the Toledo War, a lot of them contradicting one another. Not surprisingly, sympathies for the Ohio or Michigan side are often determined by who is writing the account.

At the end of the Toledo War, Congress awarded both Michigan and Ohio territory to which they weren't legally entitled. Ohio got the Toledo Strip, which should have been Michigan's, and Michigan got the western two-thirds of the Upper Peninsula, which should have been Wisconsin's. Michigan likes to say that it won the war, and Ohio had to keep Toledo as a result. Ohio likes to say that University of Michigan graduates keep their diplomas on their windshields to use as handicapped stickers. And of course, every year, the teams of the University of Michigan and Ohio State meet to fight new battles in the continuing war between Ohio and Michigan.

Forgotten Tales of Lower Michigan

Beware the Nain Rouge!

One of Michigan's greatest legends is the "Nain Rouge," the specter that shows up whenever misfortune strikes in Detroit.

It's not known exactly where the Nain Rouge came from, but early Ottawa Indian accounts mention the dread dwarf, referring to him as the "Demon from the Strait." Others say he came from Normandy, France, to the New World, specifically to Detroit.

The first recorded viewing of the Nain Rouge, whose name is French for "Red Devil," was by the founder of Detroit, Antoine Laumet de la Mothe, Sieur de Cadillac. According to the legend, Cadillac was warned by a fortuneteller to be more careful with his money and to "appease the Nain Rouge" by flattering it. He continued to live high on the hog and one day was walking home

from a May Day celebration with his wife, who spotted the dreaded dwarf.

"It is the Nain Rouge!" she exclaimed.

"Get out of my way, you red imp!" shouted Cadillac, again ignoring the fortuneteller's advice once more by swinging his cane and hitting the dwarf, which promptly vanished, laughing all the while.

This started a string of bad luck for Cadillac. Soon after, he was arrested in Montreal for abuse of authority and was reassigned to Louisiana, where he was made governor and then removed from office. From there, he returned to France, lost his fortune and was imprisoned in the Bastille for five months.

The Nain Rouge is described as a short, childlike creature (less than two and a half feet tall) with red or black fur boots, fiery red eyes and poor teeth in a constantly grinning mouth. It was said that he was seen dancing on the banks of the Detroit River on July 30, 1763, right before the Battle of Bloody Run. In this battle, fifty-eight British soldiers were killed by Native Americans from Chief Pontiac's tribe. After the battle, the small tributary of the Detroit River, which flows through what is now Elmwood Cemetery, turned red with blood and stayed bloody for days after the battle.

General Hull sighted the devilish dwarf in the morning fog during the War of 1812, right before he surrendered Fort Detroit to the British. What was particularly devilish is that General Hull didn't even surrender to a superior fighting force but was tricked into giving up the fort without a shot because he was led to believe there were many more warriors than there actually were. The militia in the fort actually greatly outnumbered the Indians, but General Hull was sure they were vastly outnumbered and didn't stand a chance. This is because that clever Indian chief Tecumseh had his men make lots of noise and march three or four times by the fort so that it looked like a lot more Indians than there actually were. Following the surrender, General Hull was relieved of command and almost executed for his incompetence. His sentence was commuted at the last minute by President Madison in honor of his Revolutionary War service. After being imprisoned for cowardice and incompetence, Hull spent the rest of his life writing books proclaiming his innocence.

All through the years, the Nain Rouge has been sighted whenever there is trouble in the area of the Motor City. On Presque Isle, a brother named Jean pestered his sister Josette to leave a mill there to him in her will. She said she would rather leave it to the devil, and sure enough, on the night she died, the mill was wrecked by a lightning bolt. The Nain Rouge was spotted in the fire.

The day before the Detroit Riot in 1967, the Nain Rouge was spotted. In 1976, right before a tremendous snow and ice storm, the dwarf was spotted on a telephone pole by two utility workers climbing the pole. They thought it was a child at first, but when they approached, the dwarf jumped from the top of the pole and disappeared.

One would think that the Nain Rouge would be seen a lot now that Detroit has declared bankruptcy. Although there has been talk of making the Nain Rouge the emergency manager of Detroit, it is generally hoped that the Nain Rouge will stay away. In fact, there is a group that can claim it is responsible for keeping Detroit free of the dreaded imp. Cadillac's fortuneteller claimed that the dwarf could be appeased through flattery. And there is now a parade in Detroit to honor (or dishonor) him—Le Marche du Nain Rouge. That has got to be about the epitome of flattery! The parade, which started in 2012, has as its purpose the banishment of the Nain Rouge. The Nain Rouge is sighted at the beginning of the parade but is soon chased out of the city by the rest of the parade. This might be the only parade in which the climax—in this case, the dreaded dwarf—is at the beginning of the parade.

STONE IDOL SACRED TO NATIVE AMERICAN GOD MANITOU DESTROYED BY FRENCH MISSIONARIES

The previous and the next few stories are based on folk tales by the earlier colonists of Michigan and the Native Americans. The following account is about half legend and half accurate.

At the island originally known as *Wah-na-be-zee*, or "Swan Island," by the Chippewa and Ottawa Indians and then called Isle Ste. Claire by the French was a monolithic stone sacred to the Native American god Manitou. It was a large stone in a clearing in the woods on top of a grassy mound. In some accounts, it was painted, and in others, it was a perfectly shaped object, polished and reflective. The local Native Americans would meditate before it and leave offerings such as buckskin, animal hides, tobacco and food. The mound was usually covered in these gifts to the god.

In 1670, a French missionary, François Dollier de Casson, and scholar Abbé Bréhant de Galinée came upon this revered object while exploring the island. Casson had been a soldier in Brittany, France, but retired to make a Christian pilgrimage for the Roman Catholic Church and to spread the word of the Lord in the New World.

Explorer Robert de la Salle had befriended one of the Iroquois Confederacy, who drew him a map showing the water routes of the Lower Michigan area. He formed an expedition to explore the area up to the Ohio River. Salle was joined by missionaries Casson and Galinée on the voyage of discovery. When Salle was taken ill, the two missionaries set off with seven others to do some exploring of the Great Lakes region.

The two explorer missionaries were in awe of the beauty of the island until they came upon the very un-Catholic-like idol. In a religious fervor, they smashed the stone and managed to drag a major portion of the rock from its pedestal. They then proceeded to use two canoes to drag the stone and dump it into the deepest part of the water. As audacious it was to destroy the Native American monument, they weren't done yet. The two missionaries then put in the place where the monolith had been a cross—with a message that said:

> *In the year of grace 1670, Clement IX being seated in the chair of St. Peter, Louis XIV reigning in France Monsieur de Corcelles being Governor of*

New France and Monsieur Talon being the intendant of the King, two missionaries of the Seminary of Montreal, accompanied by seven Frenchmen, arrived at this place and are the first of all the European people who wintered on the land bordering on Lake Erie, which they took possession of in the name of their King, as a country unoccupied, and having fixed the coat of arms of France at the foot of this cross.

François Dollier—Priest of the Diocese of Nantes, Brittany
De Galinée—Deacon of the Diocese of Rennes, Brittany

There weren't any Native American witnesses to this act of cultural vandalism and the leaving of this vainglorious document and cross, for they probably wouldn't have let the two upstart missionaries leave the area alive.

The next part of the lore is that, upon discovery of the destruction, the Native Americans took small pieces of the stone with them. The small stones led them to the large stone of Manitou in the water. The stone ordered them to put all the smaller pieces on the ground. The smaller stones then turned into snakes (in some accounts rattlesnakes), as the god said, to protect the island from further intrusion. The island was then given a new name by the French: Snake Island.

Once the French took over, they brought pigs in to control the snake population. Because of this, it was renamed Hog Island, the name it bore when it was the quarantine repository for people in the great cholera epidemic of 1832.

Hog Island is not the most elegant name for a beautiful island, so the name was changed for a fifth time to honor Belle, the lovely daughter of General Cass. The island was thereafter called Belle Isle.

If the account of the Manitou idol doesn't convince you of the reason Belle Isle was infested with snakes, the legend of the Snake Goddess of Belle Isle won't either.

The Snake Goddess was the beautiful daughter of doting father and demigod Sleeping Bear (not to be confused with the bears of Sleeping Bear Dunes). So beautiful was she, in fact, that to keep her away from prying eyes and unscrupulous suitors, her father hid her in a covered boat that swung on the Detroit River, tied to a tree on shore. However, the personification of "the Winds" saw her when Sleeping Bear went to give her some food. The

Wind then blew so hard that the cable was snapped and the boat was set free. It floated to the keeper of the water gates, who lived at the mouth of Lake Huron.

The keeper instantly fell in love with Sleeping Bear's daughter and brought her boat into his lodge. But he had just brought her in when he was attacked and killed by the Winds. He was buried on Peach Island (then known as Isle au Pêche). The keeper's spirit became an oracle, often consulted by the Native Americans before they went to war. They would fast and meditate before hearing his voice in the wind in the reeds. Before planning his campaign against the English, Pontiac fasted here for seven days.

The Winds continued its rampage and destroyed the immediate area. The canoe transformed into Belle Isle. The great Indian god Manitou, also known as the Great Spirit, placed the girl there, surrounded by snakes, to keep her safe. This is how she attained the Snake Goddess sobriquet.

The Snake Goddess is often seen transforming from a white doe into a beautiful maiden. Belle Isle visitors have reported seeing a beautiful white doe observing them from behind a bush or tree. It shyly runs when approached and, just before it disappears from sight, turns into a beautiful Indian maiden.

PONTIAC'S REBELLION AND THE FORT MICHILIMACKINAC LACROSSE GAME

Even though the French tried to convert the Native Americans to Catholicism, they got along very well with them. The two groups interacted with each other, including through marriage, to the mutual benefit of both.

During the conflict known as the French and Indian War (part of Europe's Seven Years' War between France and England), most of the Indians sided with the French to remove the English from the New World. When the English were victorious, they took over the French land claims in the New World. As the English began to settle in the area, they were less beneficent toward the Native Americans than the French had been. The main complaint against the British was the insolent attitude they had toward Native Americans—they treated the natives like slaves or dogs.

The policies instituted by General Jeffrey Amherst, the British leader in the New World, was also much despised. Amherst cut out most of the gifts previously bestowed annually on the Indian chiefs (such as tobacco, knives, guns and clothes) as awards or bribes to obtain their

cooperation in maintaining peaceful behavior. Amherst also assumed that, with the French out of the picture, the Indians had no choice but to accept less favorable British trade terms.

This brought down the ire of Ottawa chief Pontiac and almost all of the other tribes in the Midwest. After the French and Indian War in 1763, Pontiac and other tribes plotted to overthrow the English in an insurrection variously called Pontiac's War, Pontiac's Conspiracy, Pontiac's Uprising and Pontiac's Rebellion. The rebellion was first instigated by the Mingo (Seneca) chiefs Kiyasuta and Tahaiadoris, but Chief Pontiac soon took up the cause. The conflict was early on referred to as Kiyasuta and Pontiac's Rebellion, but that just didn't have the right cadence or ring to it like Pontiac's War does, so historians dropped the Kiyasuta from the name.

The tribes involved included the Chippewa, Potawatomie and Huron from the Great Lakes region and the Kickapoo, Miami, Mascouten, Weas and Piankashaw from the Illinois Country, both areas that were on friendly terms with the French settlers and wished to restore their earlier status in the New World. The Ohio country tribes—the Delaware (Lenape), Mingo (Seneca), Shawnee and Wyandot—joined the Pontiac Conspiracy because they just didn't like the British. They were especially upset about forts the British built in the area, since they figured the forts indicated that the British had warlike intentions. They also surmised that the British were limiting their access to gunpowder due to planning to battle the Native Americans. The Indians had come to depend on the gunpowder to use in hunting wild animals and providing food for their families.

On April 27, 1763, Chief Pontiac spoke to a large council of Indian tribes on the shores of the Ecorse River, in the area of present-day Lincoln Park, Michigan. Soon, the attacks on British forts began.

On May 7, Pontiac and about three hundred tribesman attacked Fort Detroit and were defeated, although a contingent of Native Americans successfully took Fort Niagara in New York. The British were defeated at the Battle of Bloody Run—in present-day Elmwood Cemetery—where the water was said to be blood red for three days after the conflict.

Battles went back and forth, and the Indian Confederacy went after smaller forts, successfully capturing Fort Sandusky near present-day Venice; Fort Ohio on Lake Erie; and Fort St. Joseph, near present-day Niles, Michigan.

To capture Fort Sandusky, members of the Wyandot tribe pretended to want to have a council meeting with the British officers. They thereby gained passage into the fort and, once inside, waged a surprise attack.

Fort Michilimackinac was at the northern tip of the Lower Peninsula, where Lake Huron and Lake Michigan meet. The subterfuge used by the Chippewa and Sauk to gain entry to Fort Michilimackinac was particularly ingenious. Although there had been rumors of tensions between the British and the Native Americans, the British had not heard of the attacks on the other forts in the area. Instead, the British were celebrating King George III's birthday on a

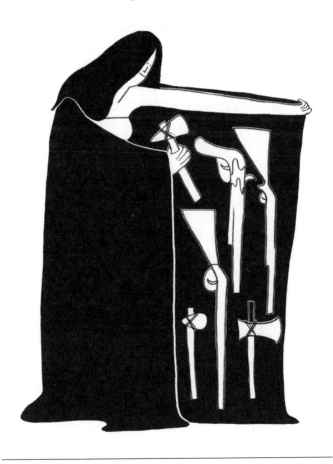

hot June 4, 1763. While celebrating, they were invited by neighboring Chippewa and Sauk Indians to watch the two teams play each other in a game of lacrosse (*baaga'adowe*) on the land in front of the fort.

Since relations with the neighboring tribes in that area had always been good, the celebrating British gave their permission to hold the game and settled back to watch. Members of both tribes and their women, who were all wrapped in big bulky blankets, came to the front of the fort to join in the festivities. The game was particularly fast-paced and spirited and went on for a while as the British continued watching and celebrating, some wagering on the outcome.

Suddenly, the ball went over the stockade walls. The jovial British let the players pass right into the fort after the ball. As they entered, the Indian sportsmen were handed guns, tomahawks and other weapons from under their women's blankets. Taking the whole garrison by surprise, the Indians took over the fort and held it for a year.

Pontiac's Rebellion ended in a draw—the Native Americans were unable to expel the British from the New World, but they did win back a lot of concessions lost when the British took over from the French.

MAD ANTHONY WAYNE NEGOTIATES THE TREATY OF GREENVILLE

Further hostilities continued after Pontiac's Rebellion as the British armed and encouraged the Native Americans to rebel against the Americans. Called the Northwest Indian War, it lasted from 1785 to 1795. The Native Americans gave the Americans some defeats before President George Washington called Revolutionary War hero Anthony Wayne back to active service. He engaged in successful battles near Toledo in the days when it was part of Michigan and led the United States' forces to victory. Wayne then negotiated the Treaty of Greenville. Once the area was securely in U.S. hands after the treaty, the land was divided into five counties, including Wayne County, named for Mad Anthony, with the seat of government in Detroit.

There are differing opinions about how Mad Anthony earned his nickname; some lean to the crazy and some to the angry type of mad. The crazy part most often is credited to his taking of Stony Point on July 16, 1778, under General George Washington's orders. That Wayne undertook the seemingly "doomed to failure" mission in the first place was considered a sign of madness. Because he undertook it with such gusto and success, with limited casualties to Wayne's forces versus many losses and prisoners taken on the British side, the mission seemed to further justify the "mad" sobriquet. On the other side, there are stories that he received the nickname because he had a very hot temper and would get boiling mad at times, especially if he sensed incompetence or if he thought there was an affront to his honor.

Another nickname Wayne received was "Dandy Wayne" because of his highly polished appearance and his insistence that his men also be well groomed—so much so, in fact, that he insisted that each company he was in charge of have an official barber to keep his men's beards and hair neatly trimmed. He stated that he "would punish any man who came to parade with a long beard, was dirty, or slovenly dressed." He wrote in a letter to General Washington that he would prefer to take well-dressed men into battle with old-fashioned swords and bayonets than to lead slovenly men owning the latest guns and weaponry. When the deprivations of Valley Forge struck, Wayne was more upset about his men not having sharp-looking uniforms than he was with them not having food. In a letter to Secretary of War Richard Peters, Wayne said, "For God's sake give us—if you can't give us anything else—give us linen."

General Wayne has many places named for him, including Wayne County in Michigan, where the Michigan territorial capital was located, and Fort Wayne, Indiana. He has *two* burial places. He died on Presque Isle in his native Pennsylvania and on his deathbed asked to be buried under the blockhouse, a request that was granted. Twelve years later, his son Isaac came from western Pennsylvania to have him exhumed to be buried in the family plot in Radnor, Pennsylvania. When the general was exhumed, he was very well preserved—he had barely decomposed at all! This unfortunately meant that the transport Isaac had brought would be too small to bring the body home. He thought he would just be fetching a "bag of bones," so to speak. A local doctor, Dr. Wallace, and four assistants provided the solution and boiled the meat from the bones of General Wayne in a big black kettle. The kettle is now on display at the museum of the Erie County Historical Society.

The bones were taken back and interred in the family plot. The boiled flesh and the innards—such as his heart, liver, et cetera—that wouldn't fit in the transport were returned to the coffin and reburied under the blockhouse. A popular legend is that son Isaac Wayne even lost some of the bones on the way to the family cemetery, and every year (around Halloween), General "Mad" Anthony Wayne comes back to retrieve the lost bones.

DETROIT SURRENDERS–WITHOUT A FIGHT!

After leaving the area following the American Revolutionary War, the British came back briefly during the War of 1812. With the help of Indian chief Tecumseh, they took Detroit without a fight. General William Hull was the territorial governor and was tricked by Indian leader Tecumseh and Sir Isaac Brock into surrendering the territorial capital of Detroit without a shot being fired—even though the colonists in the fort vastly outnumbered the attacking force.

Tecumseh had his warriors come out of the woods, circle back around the fort and then repeat this maneuver a number of times, making it appear as though there were many more warriors than there actually were. A major reason this deception worked was due to the Indians making a lot of noise. Still, when Hull waved the white flag to the British without a shot being fired, his officers were dumbfounded. Those officers included Lewis Cass and future governor of Ohio and Michigan nemesis Robert Lucas, both of whom testified at General Hull's court-martial trial. He was convicted of four counts of cowardice, seven counts of neglect of duty and "unofficer-like conduct," which shows that they were not overly concerned with grammar. For this, his sentence was death by firing squad.

Luckily for Hull, because of his age (sixty) and his Revolutionary War service, his sentence was commuted by President James Madison. Instead, he was only stripped of his rank, removed from the army rolls, branded a coward and traitor and allowed to live in disgrace for the rest of his life. Before dying in the relative safety of Newton, Massachusetts (namesake of the Fig Newton), he wrote two books proclaiming his innocence. Upon Hull's dismissal, Lewis Cass was appointed the Michigan territorial governor, and William Woodbridge was appointed territorial secretary.

Michigan—Land of Fever and Chills

An unbiased observer, looking at a map of the region of the Northwest Territories, would be hard-pressed to give an explanation for why the body of land surrounded by large, easily navigable, freshwater lakes would be nearly the last of the Northwest Territories to become an official U.S. state. This was an era when water navigation was at its peak. And yet, Ohio (1803), Indiana (1816) and Illinois (1818) all achieved statehood many years before Michigan (1837). Why would the "Water Winter Wonderland" be snubbed by early settlers?

The Michigan Territory could have used a good public relations agent. The slow settlement of Michigan was due to the poor reviews given to the area by soldiers serving in the War of 1812. They remarked that Michigan was a land "good for Indians and disease and not much else." Surveyor General Edward Tiffin did a survey of the state in 1817 and gave the glowing report that they could not find one tillable acre in the whole territory and that, besides the "worthless" soil, all they *did* find were bogs, swamps, mosquitoes, dangerous animals and savage Indians. This report even inspired a poem that was circulated along the East Coast: "Don't go to Michigan, that land of ills; the word means ague, fever and chills." (A rarely used word now, "ague" was defined as fever, chills and shaking with malaria-like symptoms.)

Other slights to Michigan came from the General Land Office, under Joseph Meigs, which stated that "hardly one acre in a thousand was fit for cultivation." When the War Department built a fort in 1822 in the area where Saginaw, Michigan, is now located, the major in charge reported that all the men, including himself, save one enlisted man, were sick with malaria. Meigs bitterly declared that only "Indians, muskrats, and bullfrogs could ever live on the Saginaw River."

OTHER MICHIGAN OBSTACLES TO SETTLEMENT

There were other obstacles to Michigan settlement besides a bad reputation as a swampy wasteland. Imagine being a "tourist" in 1839 and buying something called *The Tourist's Pocket Map of Michigan* and then having a map that has only a vague resemblance to the land.

In the days prior to the twenty-first century, maps were the Global Positioning Systems (GPS) of the day. But in 1839—two years after fighting the Toledo War and becoming a state—this was the best map that Michigan had. And this map was a big improvement over the other maps that came before it!

Surveying and mapping were not easy in the early days of the Union. About the only problem they didn't have to deal with were construction zones and malfunctioning GPS. Hostile Native Americans and disease-carrying insects were just some of the hazards encountered by surveyors. As noted, due to early reports by soldiers and surveyors, the Michigan peninsulas were avoided because the "line-runners," as surveyors were called, predicted that it would be hundreds of years before anyone would want to settle in the area, calling it a "mosquito-infested swampland." Many years later, some surveyors admitted that the stories scared them, and they often did the "running the lines" for an area in their heads, seated in a tavern, safe from the hazards they had been warned about. Consequently, for reasons both valid and due to incompetence, many of the early Michigan maps look, in retrospect, to be those of a parallel universe.

So just as sure as laughter is the best medicine when you can't afford health insurance, most of the maps of the day had inaccuracies, which was not a problem limited to explorers and new settlers. The errors also created serious problems when the inaccurate maps were used to determine state boundaries.

Conflicts in the Northwest Territory started prior to 1763, when both England and France laid claim to the area surrounding the Great Lakes. France's claim was based on Hernando de Soto's discovery of the Mississippi River in 1541. England based its claim on royal charters granted to New York, Virginia, Massachusetts and Connecticut. Of course, even if England and France hadn't both had valid claims to the area, they still would have come up with a reason to have a war, since that had been England's and

France's main preoccupation for about a thousand years. When England defeated France in the French and Indian War in 1763, England took over the Great Lakes region. When the American Revolution ended in 1783, the title to the land was transferred to the united colonies, soon to be the United States of America.

Thomas Jefferson proposed a plan, the Ordinance of 1784, to divide the new area received from the British into ten states, with each state being small enough to avoid overshadowing the small states on the East Coast like Rhode Island, Delaware and Connecticut. Michigan's Lower Peninsula would have been in the states of "Cherronesus," "Metropotamia," "Assenisipia" and "Michigania"—all names created and proposed by Jefferson. Congress never put the ordinance into effect, preferring to pass an act creating the Northwest Territory in 1787 with three to five states delineated. The name "Michigania" was the only one that stuck, becoming Michigan.

Although the United States now legally owned the area of the Northwest Territory, hostile Native Americans prevented much settlement by white pioneers until 1794. Then, General "Mad Anthony" Wayne fought the Battle of Fallen Timbers in Ohio on the Maumee River and expelled the tribes. The battle took place in a field recently hit by a storm that had knocked down many of the trees, hence the name.

MICHIGAN'S BEST PRESS AGENT: LEWIS CASS

With the bad reports and bad maps, it's little wonder that people did not at first flock to early Michigan. But once it was discovered that Michigan was not the wasteland early reports said it was, many settlers started to come via the Erie Canal, which opened in 1825. The new image was mostly due to Michigan's first territorial governor, Lewis Cass.

Lewis Cass was a Michigan supporter and represented Michigan in the U.S. Senate. While territorial governor, he took it upon himself to dispel the rumors of Michigan being the land of chills and fever. Even though he was born in Ohio, he did much to waylay the bad reputation Michigan had as a vast wasteland by actually going out and surveying the land and then reporting back on it. As an explorer, he did not appear to be the picture of physical fitness even though he was over six feet tall. The Indians referred to him as "Big Belly." But Cass and his party set out on May 24, 1820, and spent the summer exploring and surveying, covering more than 4,200 miles of unsettled wilderness. His sixty-five-person expedition, including Henry Rowe Schoolcraft, the man who named many of Michigan's counties with names he made up to sound like Indian names, traveled from Detroit across Michigan and, by birch bark canoe, went to Minnesota. After returning four months later, on September 25, Cass's reports of beautiful lakes and streams did much to contradict reports of Michigan not being habitable.

As his expedition waylaid fears about how hospitable the Michigan Territory was, a new song was born, called "Michigania," Jefferson's fanciful name for the Great Lakes area:

Michigania

Come all ye Yankee farmers—who wish to change your lot.
Who've spunk enough to travel—beyond your native spot.
And leave behind the village where Pa and Ma must stay
Come follow me, and settle in Michigania—Yea, Yea,
Yea, in Michigania.

Clearly ahead of popular styles, it popularized the "Yea, Yea, Yea" chorus a century before the Beatles did in their song "She Loves You."

The presidential runner-up in 1848, Lewis also served as secretary of state under James Buchanan, and after he was Michigan's territorial governor, he served as secretary of war in Andrew Jackson's cabinet, a position he occupied during the Toledo War.

Losing candidates and vice-presidents are rarely remembered unless it's for some other distinction, but William Butler had other local ties to Michigan, having fought in the Battle of the River Raisin, also known as the Battle of Frenchtown. When President James Monroe visited the city, it was renamed Monroe in his honor.

The battle was waged as part of the War of 1812 and actually consisted of two battles—they were between the American colonists and the British and their Native American allies. The Americans were able to force out the British in the first battle on January 18, 1813. But in a surprise rally, the British and Native Americans came back four days later and launched a counterattack that resulted in 397 Americans killed, the most slain in any War of 1812 battle. Hundreds of Americans were taken prisoner and killed—the insurrection is often called the River Raisin Massacre. Lewis Cass's future running mate, William O. Butler, was taken prisoner after the battle and sent to Fort Niagara, where he was paroled and joined the Americans in time to fight in the Battle of Thames, also known as the Battle of Moraviantown. In this decisive battle near present-day Chatham, Ontario, just across the border in Canada, Butler was cited for bravery. This battle is also the one in which the Indian leader Tecumseh was killed. The charismatic Tecumseh would probably have united the many Indian tribes into one big Native American nation if not for the settlers. He might have become so famous that today we would yell his name when jumping out of airplanes instead of "Geronimo!"

OHIO BECOMES A STATE—WITH QUESTIONABLE BOUNDARIES

In 1802, the people of the Ohio region petitioned to become a state. Part of the requirement to become a state was to declare boundary lines. But maps being what they were, and Ohioans wishing to cover themselves should their maps appear inaccurate, they added an "escape clause," the proviso to their petition that if the Northwest Ordinance boundary line fell south of the Maumee River mouth, the line was to be redrawn north of the river's mouth (with the consent of Congress).

This was because the crafty Ohioans had heard from an old hunter who knew the area well. The hunter stated that the southern tip of Lake Michigan was actually farther south than originally believed. As Ohio entered the Union in 1803, no further mention was made of this provision.

In fact, when the Northwest Territory was planned, there were more accurate maps available than the ones that were used, although it was probably not possible for the founding fathers to be sure which maps *were* the most accurate.

One of the more well-known maps of the region was the less-accurate English map known as the Mitchell map. It was crafted by nonprofessional cartographer John Mitchell, who was actually schooled in medicine and botany. Inaccuracies in the map, besides helping to spark conflict between Michigan and Ohio, also caused problems with the Georgia-Florida border with Spain. The problem with using the Mitchell map to set the Ohio border was that the map didn't take into account the Toledo Strip, a section of the country that included the towns of Port Lawrence and Vistula, soon to be combined to form Toledo. One of the best maps of the period was produced by Thomas Hutchins, known as the "Geographer to the United States of America." In spite of his fame, Congress ignored the more accurate Hutchins map in lieu of using the more circulated Mitchell map.

Hutchins also created a map of Ohio, with the sections numbered, that was very accurate. But in spite of the availability of these maps, the men who wrote the Ohio

constitution did not seek them out, perhaps because they made it too clear that the Toledo Strip should clearly go to Michigan. Instead, the framers of the constitution used the less-accurate Mitchell map. The Mitchell map was commissioned by George Montagu-Dunk, Second Earl of Halifax, who had viewed earlier maps the botanist had made. The original map's width was six feet, five inches, and the height was four feet, six inches! It was printed in eight different sheets that had all kinds of small notes on them, mostly illegible in online versions. The Mitchell map was widely distributed and originally marketed as "A Map of the British and French Dominions in North America," with the copyright date of February 13, 1755. This same map was also used to determine boundaries for the Treaty of Paris and inspired a border skirmish between Georgia and Florida, which was still owned by Spain.

Ohio did not go exactly by the book when applying to the Union. Although one of the main requirements for a territory to become a state was that it had to have sixty thousand people, Ohio was allowed to slide through with only about forty-five thousand. And unlike most states, there was no formal declaration of Ohio as a state by Congress. When this "oversight" was discovered, in 1953, a bill was introduced in the U.S. Congress by Ohio congressman George H. Bender. This bill moved to admit Ohio to the Union, retroactive to March 1, 1803, the date on which the Ohio General Assembly had first convened. It was enacted by voice vote—there isn't any record on how Michigan voted.

THE LOST VILLAGES OF VISTULA, PORT LAWRENCE, TREMAINVILLE, MANCHESTER AND LYON

Both the Michigan Territory and the State of Ohio claimed the area of Toledo. Why? Because it is situated at the mouth of the Maumee River, it was thought that the area that became Toledo would become the future metropolis that Chicago actually became.

This optimistic view was stated in 1868 in a forty-nine-page pamphlet titled *A Presentation of Causes Tending to Fix the*

Position of the Future Great City of the World in the Central Plain of North America: Showing that the Center of the World's Commerce, Now Represented by the City of London, Is Moving Westward to the City of New York and Thence, within One Hundred Years to the Best Position on the Great Lakes. Even though by the time the title was stated there wasn't much room to say anything else in the brochure, *Toledo Blade* newspaper editor Jesup Wakeman Scott stated that the center of world commerce was moving westward and that, by 1900, it would be located in TOLEDO! He thought Toledo would become bigger than the title of his pamphlet. He later revised his statement to say that Toledo would become THE LARGEST CITY IN THE WORLD. Although he voiced similar platitudes about Cincinnati and Maumee when he lived there, this time he put his money where his mouth was. He donated 160 acres to found the Toledo University of Arts and Trades, now known as the University of Toledo. The Toledo Public Library is built on land that was Jesup Scott's.

Today, Toledo is probably more well known as the point where the Ohio Turnpike and I-75 converge—an area known more for construction cones than as the place from which two states thought they could dominate the world. However, most Michiganders are so used to construction cones that they don't consider this an evil Ohio plot to keep them from entering Toledo.

Toledo was actually the combination of two—some would say three—earlier settlements. The overall area of Toledo was originally referred to as Swan Creek. A settlement named Port Lawrence was platted by Cincinnati businessmen in 1817 and then platted again in 1832, when the Panic of 1819 caused the original settlement to default. It was named for Captain James Lawrence, War of 1812 naval hero. Toledo later absorbed an early settlement known as Manchester. Vistula was the other village absorbed by Toledo when it officially was organized on January 7, 1837.

July 4, 1805, was *not* Independence Day for most of the Native American tribes of the area. This was the day a treaty was signed at "Fort Industry," which is depicted on the City of Toledo seal. In the treaty, the Native Americans agreed to vacate the area for a small sum of money.

Many accounts mention that there is little record of Fort Industry other than in the treaty. There are no accounts of what became of the fort other than that it was little more than a trade depot because of the presence of nearby Fort Miami and Fort Meigs. Was there a fire? Was the fort torn down? Fort Industry Square in present-day Toledo is devoid of anything portraying a fort. Perhaps the settlers were so embarrassed about the one-sided agreement signed with the Native Americans, including the Wyandot, Ottawa, Chippewa, Munsee, Delaware, Potawatomi and Shawnee tribes, that they got rid of any reminders, including Fort Industry.

The treaty stated that the United States would pay $825.00 "every year forever hereafter, in Detroit, or some other convenient place for the ceded lands south of the 41st degree of north latitude, and an additional $175.00 for [an area called] the Firelands, which lie north of 41 degrees north." They apparently must not have found a "convenient place" because the money wasn't paid as promised, and this treaty moved the Native Americans of the area farther west. So the Native Americans signed over to the settlers a half million acres of land south of Lake Erie and west of the Cuyahoga River in northeastern Ohio for basically nothing.

What is known about Fort Industry was that it was in the Port Lawrence area of Toledo and was built as a French trading post around 1670, later coming into the possession of the British until they stopped using it in 1796. U.S. troops rebuilt it as a fort between 1800 and 1803. Because there were two forts just a few miles away—Fort Meigs and Fort Miami—Fort Industry became more of an outpost and disappeared after 1843.

Also on the city seal is the city's cryptic Latin motto, *Laborare Est Orare*, which translates as: "To Work Is to Pray." Early day Toledo, like Michigan, could have used a better public relations firm. Since it has a structure known as Fort Industry and the motto "To Work Is to Pray" pictured on its official seal, Toledo unfortunately sounds more like a labor camp than a place to settle and raise a family.

Vistula was platted and organized in 1833 by Major Benjamin F. Stickney and Edward Bissell when they didn't feel the growth of Port Lawrence was rapid enough, considering there was a railroad and canal coming through. Port Lawrence, Fort Industry and Vistula were combined to form the city of Toledo. Major Stickney was destined to play a key role in the history of Toledo—in more ways than one.

Benjamin Franklin Stickney was born in 1773 in Pembroke, New Hampshire, and married Mary Stark, daughter of military hero General John Stark. Named for Benjamin Franklin, Stickney possessed a silver tankard that was said to have been given to the family by Benjamin Franklin himself. Handed down to various heirs, the tankard was donated to the Toledo Museum of Art in 1915. It was openly displayed until research showed that the tankard had been made in 1797, seven years after Ben Franklin died. It has since been put into storage.

The area around Toledo had been settled before Toledo, mainly due to the uncertainty of whether the Toledo area was in the territory of Michigan or the state of Ohio. The nearby settlement of Manchester, later absorbed by Toledo, was prospering and had a newspaper in 1832. Perrysburg was the largest Ohio settlement near Toledo. It was a small settlement in 1813, when General (later, president) William Henry Harrison ordered the construction of Fort Meigs during the War of 1812. Located across the Maumee River from the ruins of the old British Fort Miami and near the site of the 1794 Battle of Fallen Timbers, Fort Meigs survived two major sieges. In the first siege, the fort was held through the help of Kentucky reinforcements, led by Colonel William Dudley, many of whom were slaughtered by British-sympathizing Native Americans in an engagement known as Dudley's Massacre. The Americans held out, helped by "Miller's Charge," in which Colonel John Miller, leading a group of 350 men, disabled the British big guns and captured 40 prisoners.

By the Second Siege, General Harrison had left, and the fort had been downgraded to a supply depot. In the Second Siege, the Native American contingent staged a phony battle outside the fort to try to lure the Americans out while the British snuck in. Not falling for it, the Americans dug in and stuck it out. After the British left the area, General Harrison ordered the fort dismantled.

Perrysburg, named for War of 1812 naval hero Oliver Hazard Perry, was the gathering place for Ohio troops during the Toledo War. In 1816, Major Pierre Charles L'Enfant, who is famous for platting Washington, D.C., surveyed and platted the area. Perrysburg was one of the only two cities to be platted by the federal government (the nation's capital being the other).

Down the Maumee River, Waterville was founded in 1831. Defiance was founded in 1794, when Fort Defiance was built by Mad Anthony Wayne as a defense post during the battles with Native Americans. Napoleon, Ohio, between Perrysburg and Defiance, was founded in 1832. It was named for Napoleon Bonaparte by founder Elnathan Corey, a big Napoleon enthusiast. In 1836, Corey also laid out two towns named for famous battles of Napoleon: Marengo and Austerlitz. Unfortunately, he might as well have named them Waterloo and Trafalgar because both communities failed after a short time.

Napoleon Bonaparte sold the Louisiana Purchase, much of which became the Northwest Territories, to the United States. President Thomas Jefferson sent surveyors Meriwether Lewis and William Clark out to explore the area in 1803.

Napoleon is often pictured in his "hand-in-waistcoat" pose that seems to have started a nineteenth-century craze. It has been said that he had heartburn when this portrait was painted or that he was hiding his snuff. One popular theory is that artists just found it more difficult and time-consuming than it was worth to draw hands. A number of scholars say that he is giving the Masonic sign of Master of the Second Veil. Because the Masonic Order had numerous members in high places, many people were opposed to the Masons. This opposition led to a political party with even less of a sense of humor than the Whigs—the Anti-Masons.

Before platting Vistula and waging war against Michigan, Major Benjamin Stickney's career got a big boost when he married the daughter of General John Stark in 1802. General Stark served in the French and Indian War, during which he planned an attack on the English at Fort William Henry in March 1757. He knew the regiment of soldiers stationed there was from Ireland and calculated that they would have celebrated St. Patrick's Day the day before. He was right. The regulars were too hung over to wage war, and Stark's troops easily took the fort.

In the American Revolutionary War, General Stark outwitted British troops, attacking Massachusetts from along

the Mystic River. Through stealth and cleverness (he was able to "mystically" conceal his New Hampshire troops behind a stone wall, hiding them until it was too late for the British to retreat from the battle), he was responsible for the British losing 40 percent of their men. Stark was the last surviving Revolutionary War general, living to the age of ninety-four. General Stark was Major Stickney's father-in-law.

Major Stickney married Mary Stark when he was the ripe old age of twenty-nine, which, despite General Stark's advanced age, was considered middle age in the 1800s. Marrying the daughter of a noted war hero proved to be a good move for Ben Stickney. Through his connections to General Stark, he became the postmaster and justice of the peace of Pembroke, New Hampshire. He was also asked to carry on some successful spying missions to count Canadian troops during the War of 1812. His actions helped to forestall a possible invasion of Canada by the Americans. It was during this war that he gained the unofficial rank of major. (Even though it was "unofficial," this did not keep him from using the title for the rest of his life.) Through these journeys, he first encountered the Maumee River Valley. Following a stint in Fort Wayne, Indiana, as an Indian agent, he moved to the Maumee River Valley in 1820.

In many ways, Major Stickney was the main impetus behind the Toledo War. At a public meeting that he called in 1821, he said that the citizens of the area would benefit more under the protection of the United States government as part of the Michigan Territory and that all they would get from being part of the state of Ohio was taxed. Stickney later stated in his autobiography, printed in the *Toledo Blade* newspaper, that he had masterminded the Toledo War and helped Ohio win by goading Michigan into committing hostilities against Ohioans.

Considered a nutcase by many and merely eccentric by others, Major Stickney's peculiar character was evidenced by his naming his two sons One and Two, ostensibly so that they could choose their own names later. However, each son chose to keep just the number for a first name, as Two Stickney's tombstone in Forest Cemetery (on Stickney Avenue) in Toledo shows.

Interestingly, Two Stickney has been credited with the naming of Toledo. His class was studying Spain, which has a famous city named Toledo, and Two informed the naming committee that no other place in the New World was using the name Toledo.

Ben Stickney would have named all his daughters after states of the Union but was stopped by his wife, Mary. He did name his third daughter Indiana, the state where she was born. But despite these and other eccentricities, Major Stickney had his followers. In 1821, he was able to convince his neighbors that it was to their advantage, tax wise, to "secede" from Ohio and to say they were in Michigan so they could pay the less costly Michigan taxes. Major Stickney even cemented his Michigan claim by becoming a Michigan justice of the peace and postmaster. However, as the overall pictured changed, in 1823, he was able to convince his neighbors that a successful future for them would be more likely as citizens of Ohio because it was already a state of the Union. Ben Stickney took this view because he had a number of irons in the fire after moving to the Maumee River area. He had purchased land and had invested in the Wabash and Erie Canal project, which planned to expand to the Ohio area by linking Lake Erie with the Ohio River.

One of the chief reasons for Toledo being formed from Port Lawrence and Vistula was to have a larger inhabited area, providing more reason for the canal to have a terminus close by. Hedging his transportation bets, Major Stickney was also a supporter of the Lake Erie and Kalamazoo Railway, which would be bringing a railroad connection from Adrian, Michigan, to the Toledo area. He felt that it would be more likely for progress, in the form of canals and railroads, to come if the area was in a state of the Union instead of a mere territory, like Michigan.

Major Stickney found out that the canal terminus would be built at Perrysburg instead of the Toledo area, and this was when he switched allegiances from Michigan to Ohio and convinced his neighbors that they needed to be considered part of Ohio in order to not lose out on canal profits. Although he was considered strange, his neighbors recognized him as a very intelligent man. He had learned twenty different Native American dialects and had published Native American dictionaries, as well as other works. He wrote newspaper articles and editorials (he was a co-founder of the *Toledo Blade* newspaper), many of them criticizing government officials for their poor treatment of Native Americans. Besides government work, he was a successful real estate speculator. In later years, Stickney Elementary School and downtown Toledo landmark Stickney Hall carried his name. Stickney Avenue runs past Forest Cemetery in Toledo, located on land that Benjamin Stickney donated, where he and his son Two are buried. Both father and son Two would achieve their greatest fame in connection to the events leading up to the Toledo War.

"Future Great City" Toledo had opposing forces in each state who wished to be the ones to control the city. In the Michigan Territory, hopes were high that a new road from Detroit to Toledo, being constructed by the territorial government, would increase prosperity for each area. Also, with the Lake Erie and Kalamazoo Railway coming through, Toledo would be an important link. Another consideration was that the Toledo Strip gave the owner access to Lake Erie.

For Ohioans, the Wabash and Erie Canal project was the impetus to make Toledo the property of Ohio. In 1812, Amos Stafford submitted a petition with the signatures of fifty families living in the disputed area. They claimed that they felt themselves to be Ohioans and were opposed to the Michigan laws under which they were living. Predictably, local survey results often depended on who was taking the survey because another survey had the residents voting to be in Michigan. In any regard, the Act of 1812 was passed by the U.S. legislature, which called for a resurveying of the line. However, Michigan had been governing the territory; the residents had been voting in Michigan elections; and the residents, for the most part, considered themselves part of Michigan.

The Toledo area had five post offices originally founded as part of the Michigan Territory that were in the disputed territory. Tremainville was founded in 1825 by brothers Isaac and Calvin Tremain and was transferred to Lucas County, Ohio, in 1835. Port Lawrence was considered part of Monroe County in the Michigan Territory (or MT, as it was written on addresses), and its first post office was known as Depot, with Benjamin F. Stickney, future founder of Vistula, becoming the first postmaster on December 1, 1823. The name of the post office was changed to Port Lawrence on October 7, 1825, to honor War of 1812 hero Commodore Oliver Hazard Perry, who won the Battle of Lake Erie on the Great Lakes. Perry's ship was named the *Lawrence*. (Perrysburg, Ohio, was also named in honor of Oliver Perry.) Settlers writing letters to one another were not sure which state the area would be in. At least one letter was noted to be addressed to the "State of Confusion."

In 1832, the Michigan Territorial Legislative Council authorized a road to be built from Vistula to Detroit. The Vistula post office was organized in 1834 and operated as a Michigan territorial post office for one year. Manhattan in the Toledo Strip established a post office in February 1836, with Daniel Chase as the postmaster. The area was ceded to Ohio and made part of Lucas County. It is now within the city limits of Toledo. Another village was Lyons, now one mile from the Michigan border in Ohio. Because it was located in the Toledo Strip, it, too, considered itself to be part of Michigan until the Toledo War.

MAP GAP LEADS TO FLAP

Many of the forgotten tales of Michigan tell about the complications leading up to its becoming a state and how a much-heralded rivalry with Ohio began, one that continues to this day. The roots of the rivalry began with a 468-square-mile strip of land at the edge of the Maumee River. The land, which became known as the Toledo Strip, was at first governed by Michigan. The Northwest Ordinance of 1787 established the boundary between Ohio and Michigan as an east–west line drawn from the southern tip of Lake Michigan across the base of the peninsula. The original line was drawn using maps that showed it intersecting Lake Erie north of the Maumee River. Later, maps that were more accurate included an area around the Maumee River, which was not originally shown on the earlier maps. Eventually, these simple map errors led to the most rabid state rivalry ever between two U.S. states.

In 1825, the Erie Canal opened, and "canal fever" hit the land. Ohio took much more interest in the Toledo Strip than it had before. In fact, it took so much interest that it became involved with the Michigan Territory in a conflict that became known as the Toledo War, which led to today's Michigan-Ohio rivalry.

Michigan knew it was in for a fight over its border with Ohio. The fact that Ohio was a bona fide state while Michigan was still a territory did not help matters. So when Andrew Jackson came to office in 1829, the Michigan territorial legislature attempted to curry favor with the new administration, naming nine counties after members of Jackson's cabinet. They were named for President Andrew Jackson, Vice President John C. Calhoun, Secretary of State Martin Van Buren (and later Secretary of State Edward Livingston), Secretary of the Treasury Samuel D. Ingham, Postmaster General William T. Barry, Attorney General John M. Berrien, Secretary of the Navy John Branch and Secretary of War John Eaton. Lewis Cass, soon to become secretary of war in July 1831, also had a county named for him, as did Chancellor James Kent, a New York lawyer and legal counsel for Michigan during the Toledo War affair.

Nine counties of Michigan have names that explorer Henry Lowe Schoolcraft, who was also an Indian agent and author, made up to sound like Native American names. These invented names were usually adapted from parts of Native American words, but they sometimes had parts with Greek, Arabic and Latin roots. These counties are: Alcona, Allegan, Alpena, Arenac, Iosco, Kalkaska, Leelanau, Oscoda and Tuscola.

Of the eighty-three counties in Michigan, twenty-nine are named for people, and twenty-two are named for rivers, lakes or other features that already had names, like Muskegon for the Muskegon River or Huron for Lake Huron. Other counties were given basic geographic names, like Bay County and Hillsdale County. Many of the county names were the names of tribes, such as Menominee, Ottawa and Chippewa, and some were the names of Indian chiefs, including Osceola, Sanilac, Ogemaw, Mecosta, Newaygo and Missaukee. Four counties were named for Irish locales:

Antrim, Clare, Roscommon and Wexford. Another county was named Emmett County for Robert Emmett, an Irish patriot hanged by the British. And Schoolcraft named one county for himself. He at least didn't try to be transparent about it like Judge Augustus Woodward, who named many streets of Detroit after various settlers yet claimed he named the main street of Detroit Woodward Avenue not for himself but because it went "toward the woods."

The naming of the counties for Jackson cabinet members did little to influence the Ohio-Michigan border question in Michigan's favor, probably because 1) the cabinet members had little to do with the governing of the Northwest Territories; 2) President Jackson was known to listen to his "Kitchen Cabinet," an informal group of his political cronies, more than he listened to his actual cabinet; and 3) all but one of Jackson's cabinet resigned in response to the "Eaton Affair," also known as the "Petticoat Affair."

The Eaton Affair began when Secretary of State John Eaton married Margaret "Peggy" O'Neale Timberlake. Peggy had an unsavory reputation due to rumors of her being sexually promiscuous with patrons of her family's tavern, O'Neale's, while her alcoholic naval officer husband, Timberlake, was out at sea. When Timberlake killed himself, Eaton married Peggy on January 1, 1829. The other cabinet wives refused to associate with her and wouldn't invite her to tea or any cabinet wife activities. President Jackson was already sensitive to these types of social issues because of the turmoil regarding his marriage to his late wife, Rachel. Rachel's ex-husband had not filed their divorce papers as he had promised. When she married Jackson, her marital status surfaced, and she was accused of bigamy. In regards to the Eaton affair, President Jackson ordered the wives to stop shunning and instead befriend Peggy Eaton. The wives refused, which eventually led to most of the cabinet members who had just had Michigan counties named for them—including Berrien, Branch, Calhoun and Ingham—resigning their posts. Obviously, most of the Michigan counties had already ordered their business cards and stationery, so they kept the names.

WOULD YOU TRUST A CONFEDERATE GENERAL TO MAP YOUR STATE BOUNDARY?

Because of the map irregularities of the day, both the Michigan Territory and the State of Ohio felt they owned the area surrounding Toledo, dubbed the Toledo Strip. Two surveys had been conducted; one, called the Harris Line for its surveyor, was arranged by former Ohio governor Edward Tiffin, with orders to survey the line according to the Ohio Constitution. When this line came back as expected, with the Toledo Strip in Ohio, Lewis Cass protested. A second line was ordered, called the Fulton Line after its surveyor. This line was to be determined using the specifications of the Northwest Territory. It placed the Toledo Strip in the Michigan Territory.

Agitation over the Ohio-Michigan boundary lines continued, including "irregularities" found in the Fulton line, so in 1832, Congress passed a law providing for a *third* survey of the ordinance line to be completed by December 31, 1835. Conducting the survey would be Andrew Talcott, captain of the Army Corps of Engineers, the same person who had done the hatchet job on Michigan many years earlier, helping to spread the "mosquito-infested swamp wasteland" story of why people shouldn't settle there.

Doing the actual work were army lieutenants Washington Hood and Robert E. Lee, the very same Robert E. Lee who would lead the Confederate forces during the upcoming American Civil War. The line was completed in June 1834, a year and a half sooner than expected, and the results coincided with the Fulton line, supporting Michigan's claim to the area. However, Congress would still not relent on supporting Michigan's statehood petition until the border matter was fully settled. Pouring gasoline on the fire was an Ohio congressman who stated that since Michigan would always be a third- or fourth-rate power due to its population and geography, he could see no reason to discuss the boundary issue at all.

Andrew Talcott, the leader of the third band of surveyors, came from an old Connecticut family that included Joseph Talcott, governor of the colony of Connecticut from 1724 to 1741, and John Talcott, a founder of Hartford, Connecticut. Andrew attended West Point and was friends with Robert E. Lee, who tried their friendship when Lee asked him to be state engineer of Virginia during the Civil War. Unfortunately, this position also placed him in charge of the defense of Richmond and the James River and Fort Boykin. This was a job he miserably failed at when Richmond was bombarded and lost to the North. He fled to New York, where he was arrested in March 1863, only to be held at Fort Warren in Massachusetts as a *Mexican* citizen. How did an American surveyor who attended West Point happen to become a Mexican citizen? Talcott had been chief engineer and superintendent of the Ohio and Mississippi Railroad (he had to testify before a coroner's jury regarding the Desjardins Canal Bridge railway accident in Hamilton, Ontario, in 1857, in which fifty-nine people were killed and many more injured) and was commissioned to help with a railroad line being built from Veracruz to Mexico City. (Apparently, it didn't take much for Mexico to give citizenship to a foreigner.)

Many words have been written about General Robert E. Lee, leader of the Confederate military forces during the Civil War. Although many people know his horse's name (Traveler) and his last words ("Strike the tent"), few people know he had been a surveyor or that he was a first cousin, once removed, to Helen Keller. On this surveying expedition, he revealed his little-known sense of humor when he mentioned stopping at the Pelee Island Lighthouse and "killing the keeper" of the light. In further reading of Lee's journal, the keeper of the lighthouse is found to be a snake.

Surprisingly, Lee was not the most famous person to be a surveyor. George Washington, Thomas Jefferson and Abraham Lincoln, three out of four of the presidents depicted on Mount Rushmore, were surveyors. Lewis and Clark were sent to survey the Louisiana Purchase land that Napoleon sold to the United States. Lewis Cass, as previously mentioned, surveyed parts of the Michigan Territory to prove that it wasn't uninhabitable. Mad Anthony Wayne also did some surveying. Surveyors had the power to create political boundaries, which would cause skirmishes and all-out wars. After explorers discovered an area, the very next people to follow would be the surveyors, the real estate agents of their day. Many lakes, rivers and other geographic regions (such as Lake Burt in Michigan, named for William Burt) are named for surveyors.

William Burt was one of the original surveyors of the Northwest Territory and lived in Mount Vernon, Michigan, in Macomb County. He was multitalented, inventing and receiving a patent for the first typewriter, which he called a typographer (the prototype is in the Smithsonian Institution in Washington, D.C.). He also invented the solar compass. This would allow surveyors to use the position of the sun when a regular compass wouldn't work. Burt developed the compass when faced with iron deposits in Michigan that interfered with the magnetic properties of a regular compass.

The other surveyor in the Talcott party was Washington Hood, mapmaker, who was the 500th graduate of West

Point. Unfortunately, many of his maps were controversial. Hood's maps were said to be inaccurate and might even have been plagiarized. In a book published in 1846, Wyndham Robertson's *Oregon: Our Right and Title*, Hood's map of the Oregon Territory shows the Great Salt Lake to be rectangular!

So, the Talcott line, done to the Northwest Ordinance specifications, showed that Michigan's version of the boundary was correct. But it was ignored! Ohio declared its intention of doing the line yet again. This was not appreciated by the Michiganders—especially their new "boy governor," Stevens T. Mason.

DON'T CALL MASON THE BOY GOVERNOR!

Lewis Cass had resigned as Michigan governor in 1831, when he was named secretary of war in Jackson's cabinet. John Thomson Mason was named territorial secretary, while George Porter was made territorial governor. In the absence of the governor, the territorial secretary acted as governor.

The Masons were an old Virginia family. John T. Mason's granduncle George Mason wrote the original Virginia Constitution, which heavily influenced the U.S. version. Stevens T. Mason, father of John T. Mason and namesake of John's son, Stevens Mason, was a senator representing Virginia in the U.S. Senate from 1794 until his death in 1803. Andrew Jackson was a visitor to the Mason home and knew the young Stevens, known as Tom, from an early age.

President Jackson believed in the adage "to the victor go the spoils" and was the first president to widely use his powers to fire officials who did not support him—in that day, usually members of the Whig Party. The Whigs were considered a more gentile, conservative and moneyed party than the grass-roots Democratic Party of Andy Jackson. After the firings, Jackson would then appoint his supporters to the positions vacated. In this manner, John T. Mason became territorial secretary, taking over for William Woodbridge.

In the early territorial governments, when the governor of the region was out of the area, the secretary became acting governor. President Jackson sent John Mason on a mission to Texas, probably to test the waters of the independent Lone Star Texas government to see if it was interested in joining the United States. John Mason's nineteen-year-old son, Stevens, had been helping him with his duties, so when John Mason left, Jackson appointed Stevens to be territorial secretary. President Jackson appointed George Porter as governor in 1831, but Porter did not care for the state much and was absent most of the time. In one message, it is stated that he had been in the territory for three weeks out of the last five months, and in another, it stated that he had been gone for eight months. This left most of the governing to Stevens Mason.

In one letter to Jackson, Stevens asks for more money since Porter was never there and yet collected the full governor's salary while Mason did all the work. As mentioned, Stevens Thomson Mason was only nineteen when he assumed the job but had already been helping his father navigate the rough waters of Michigan politics for a year since arriving in Michigan. He did most of the writing for his father, having attended Transylvania University before coming to Michigan.

Although Porter was rarely in the state, he unfortunately chose to make one of his rare appearances during a serious cholera outbreak that would go on to kill, according to many estimates, 10 percent of the population. When Porter died in the cholera epidemic of July 1834, the territorial secretary, Stevens Mason, assumed the office of (acting) territorial governor of Michigan.

Mason was instantly popular in the state even though he had a volatile temper. He did not like being called the "boy governor" or, as President Andrew Jackson referred to him, the "young hotspur." Another nickname he didn't like was "the Stripling"; in fact, the only moniker he would accept was Tom.

A newspaper editor, George Corselius, of a Whig-leaning Ann Arbor newspaper, the *Western Emigrant*, called him "Boy Governor" in an article. When Mason saw the editor on Jefferson Avenue in Detroit a week later, they had an energetic discussion in which Corselius insulted Mason's father. This led to a tussle, in which Mason gave Corselius "a severe cuffing, which from all accounts warmed his ears," according to the rival newspaper, the *Ann Arbor Argus*, which did not tire of bringing up this incident. Mason apparently got into three different fistfights in the space of two weeks and had to post a $500 bond. His main opponents within the local government would continue to be members of the Whig Party.

The Whigs were an early political party that elected two presidents of the United States: William Henry Harrison and Zachary Taylor. Two other Whigs became president when both of the two elected Whigs died in office. The two vice presidents who became "accidental presidents" were John Tyler and Millard Fillmore. The Whigs started from the remains of the Anti-Mason Party, who weren't formed to oppose Stevens Mason and his kin but rather to oppose freemasonry, which many feared was plotting to overthrow the government. The Whigs did not make the most fortunate choices for presidential candidates. Their first winner, famed general William Henry Harrison, was an Indian fighter who talked too long in the cold during his inauguration address and died of pneumonia one month into his term—a record for the shortest presidency that will be tough to beat. His successor was Vice President John Tyler, who set the precedent for the vice president to be the president upon the death of the president and not just "acting president." When Tyler received documents declaring him acting president, he crossed out the "acting" portion. He refused to follow the agenda of the Whigs and was soon abandoned by the whole Whig Party. Usually when a person is president already, he is considered the front-runner for the party's nomination to continue his term for another four years. But Tyler wasn't even nominated.

The other Whig candidate to win an election was famed general Zachary Taylor, who also died in office, just a year and a half into his term, not saying much for the longevity of Whig generals elected president. He was succeeded by Millard Fillmore, whose most notable achievement is usually attributed to his wife, First Lady Abigail, who established the first library in the Executive Mansion. Fillmore was the last Whig president and ended up so unpopular over passing the Fugitive Slave Act that, *again*, the Whig Party wouldn't renominate its own sitting president! He ended up running for president under the Know-Nothing (or American) Party in 1856. That party obviously knew nothing about Fillmore's unpopularity when it nominated him—he came in dead last. However, not knowing about Fillmore's lack of popularity *did* give more credibility to the Know-Nothing Party's name.

So to sum up, the Whig Party elected two presidents, the two with the shortest terms. These presidents were succeeded by vice presidents not even renominated by the party. Is it any wonder the Whigs were a defunct political party before mid-century?

In Michigan, the dominant party was Lewis Cass's Democratic Party, descended from Thomas Jefferson's party and continued by Andrew Jackson as Jacksonian

Democrats. Mason was also a Democrat, and his main opposition, besides Governor Lucas of Ohio, was Michigan Whig leader William Woodbridge, later the second governor of Michigan. Woodbridge had been territorial secretary when Lewis Cass was the governor and had often, like Mason, acted as governor in Cass's absence. He was also elected the first territorial representative to the U.S. Congress for the Michigan Territory in 1819. Woodbridge was not so much a political opponent to Mason as he was an archenemy in the manner of Robin Hood versus the Sheriff of Nottingham, Sherlock Holmes versus Professor Moriarty and Lex Luther versus Superman. Woodbridge bitterly resented Stevens Mason taking over for him as territorial secretary. When Michigan's constitution was being written, Woodbridge tried to insert a clause limiting the governorship to men over thirty, a ploy to keep the twenty-five-year-old Mason ineligible. During Mason's final days in Michigan, Woodbridge hounded Mason relentlessly on trumped-up accusations and even admitted that he hoped to somehow manipulate Mason into a prison term.

Especially for one barely in his mid-twenties, Mason conducted himself with honor in three different "wars" in just six years. These were the Black Hawk, Toledo and Patriot Wars. In the eventful year of 1832, after taking on the duties of the governor, he ordered out the Michigan militia during the Black Hawk War. Major General John R. Williams, who was sympathetic to

Woodbridge and the Whigs, ignored the first call-to-arms order from Mason. When it appeared that Williams was also ignoring his second order, Mason had the order to call out the militia published in the *Detroit Free Press.* This woke up Williams enough to actually finally call out the militia. Williams and Woodbridge later kicked up a fuss, stating the militia was not needed in the two-month war—even though it was great public relations for Michigan since there were many reports of the valor of the Michigan militia. The Michigan militia served with distinction in this war against sixty-year-old Black Hawk, a Native American Sauk warrior who recruited enough fellow Native Americans among the Sauk, Winnebago and Potawami tribes in the area to give the Americans a lot of trouble in Illinois from May to June 1832.

Future president Abraham Lincoln was a soldier in the Black Hawk War and in fact was elected captain of his company. But the closest he got to any conflict was wrestling another soldier for a prime camping spot (he lost). One time, when Captain Lincoln was drilling his men, he came to a gate and couldn't remember the command to get his men through. So he ordered them to halt and re-form on the other side of the gate in two minutes. Honest Abe also mentioned that though he didn't see combat, he did have a lot of bloody encounters with mosquitoes but never fainted for loss of blood.

Before the cholera epidemic in 1834 that killed Governor Porter, there was a cholera epidemic in 1832, wiping out an estimated 10 percent of the population of Detroit. When Governor Mason had business in the quarantine area on Hog Island (now called Belle Isle, where many of the cholera victims were taken to either recover or die), he was arrested by a constable who could not believe a youngster like him would be conducting any kind of important business. He started to believe it the next day when the youngster had him fired.

Also in 1832, Michigan took a vote to see how many people were interested in entering the Union as a state, and the admission advocates won by 1,817 to 1,190. Therefore, Mason submitted the first petition to Congress to start the process of Michigan's statehood. When it was ignored, Mason had a territorial census conducted. The census, completed in 1834, showed that Michigan had 85,856 people—just in the Lower Peninsula. This was nearly 26,000 more than the 60,000 needed to become a state. The territorial council then petitioned Congress for an "enabling act" to permit Michigan to call a constitutional convention. However, leaned on by the Ohio delegation, Congress refused the request because of the Toledo Strip boundary question between Ohio and Michigan.

The favorable (to Michigan) results of the Talcott survey were announced in June 1834. Soon after taking office, Mason called a special session of the territorial legislature to expedite the entry of Michigan into the Union as a state. In November, he spoke before the legislature about the importance of Michigan keeping the Toledo Strip. The legislature supported Mason by authorizing him to appoint three commissioners to negotiate the ordinance line with commissioners from Ohio, Indiana and Illinois. However, all three states declined to negotiate with Michigan. Ohio governor Robert Lucas took a particularly imperious attitude and thought that an official state in the Union had no business negotiating with a mere territory. He figured the problem was between the State of Ohio and the federal government, not the Michigan Territory.

In January 1835, Stevens Mason again addressed the legislature and, despite being refused an enabling act by the U.S. Congress, arranged for Michigan to hold a constitutional convention in Detroit on the second Monday of May 1835.

Mason was very aware of public opinion and was well supported by the people of the Michigan Territory at the time of the Toledo War hostilities. He was not above trying to influence opinion by anonymously penning letters to the local newspapers of the day. He used the pen name Aristides, whom Herodotus the historian said was "the best and most honorable man in Athens." Although Mason hoped that this is how the people of Michigan would think of him, many figured out that he was the Aristides writing letters to the newspapers.

PAINS AND PENALTIES ACT: FIVE YEARS AT HARD LABOR

In 1835, when Ohio governor Robert Lucas heard that Michigan planned to hold a convention to become a state—before settling the border question with Ohio over the northern border—he took action, especially when he learned that the new state of Michigan's boundaries would be including the Toledo Strip area.

Robert Lucas was born in Virginia and served in the War of 1812. He gained prominence when he presented evidence in the court-martial trial of General William Hull of Hull's incompetence in giving Detroit and the Michigan Territory to the British without a fight. Elected to the Ohio Senate (like a previous brother), in 1818 he became Speaker of the state senate. He served as the chairman and president of the first Democratic National Convention in 1831 and in 1832 became governor of Ohio.

When Lucas informed the Ohio legislature of Michigan's statehood convention intentions, the legislature voted to officially extend Ohio's jurisdiction to include the Toledo Strip. The Michigan Territorial Legislative Council responded by passing the Pains and Penalties Act on February 12, 1835. Stevens T. Mason wrote the resolution, imposing fines of $1,000 or five years in prison at HARD LABOR on anyone other than the proper Michigan authorities attempting to exercise a "foreign jurisdiction" in the Toledo Strip.

One account has 1,160 volunteers joining the Second Michigan Volunteer Regiment, as it was named. This included 140 Monroe County men, led by Warner Wing, and 61 in the Light Horse Company, led by Captain and Deputy Sheriff Joseph Wood. Another account has Mason short on volunteers and attempting to draft 500 more men. Mason wrote to President Jackson on March 5, 1835, and requested two companies of regulars to be sent from Fort Gratiot to occupy the border region. Jackson asked his attorney general, Benjamin Butler, to rule on whether the Pains and Penalties Act was legal and was assured by Butler that "all the right is on the side of the Territory of Michigan and Ohio has no rights of jurisdiction north of the Fulton line."

To arm his militias, Mason requested one thousand muskets and seventy-five thousand cartridges from the U.S. Arsenal in Detroit. Colonel Henry Whiting, acting quartermaster, didn't ask for approval from the higher-ups in Washington because he thought the request was too urgent to wait for word from above. Although Whiting immediately filled most of the order, he refused to give Mason the cannons he wanted. When former territorial secretary of war Lewis Cass heard about the arms being distributed, he ordered Whiting to retrieve the weapons immediately.

Mason knew he might need some experienced military men soon and appointed Brigadier General Joseph Brown of the Third U.S. Brigade to be the head of the army. General Brown led the Michigan forces during the Black Hawk War and was honored for his leadership. Brown was a founder of Tecumseh, Michigan, often the meeting place for the Michigan militia during the Toledo War. Brown was a Michigan supporter through and through, remarking that anyone trying to exercise authority in the strip other than Michigan "would have to march over the dead bodies of that portion of her citizens who had heretofore been under the jurisdiction of Michigan." General Brown then called up three brigades for immediate military service.

Other than being named after an Indian chief who was a major opponent of the Americans, this is not the most notorious trivia about the small town of Tecumseh. This small, unfortunate village was also the habitat of not one but two of the deadliest serial killers ever. On May 18, 1927, Andrew Phillip Kehoe, who was born and raised in Tecumseh, bombed a school building in Bath, Michigan, killing over forty and injuring more than fifty people. This was called the Bath School Disaster and is one of the first terrorist bombings. Henry Lee Lucas (no direct relation to Ohio governor Robert Lucas) killed his mother in Tecumseh and began his string of more than two hundred reputed murders.

Brigadier General Brown was aided by Alpheus Felch, who went on to become governor of Michigan in 1846 and 1847. Felch's Toledo War service and patriotism were surprisingly not used much in his campaign. Well, "never mentioned" would probably be more accurate.

The war talk between the two sides included Ohio governor Lucas being told that he would have to "march over the dead bodies" of his troops. Lucas said that he would prevail in holding the land for Ohio even if he had to "wade knee-deep in blood." In 1827, when Michigan first began to govern the area of the Toledo Strip, in an effort to compromise, Michigan had offered Ohio the land east of the Maumee while it would retain the land north and west of the river. Ohio refused the offer. After the events of early April 1835, Mason offered again to meet with Governor Lucas to settle their sectional divisions. Lucas refused the offer, saying that Mason's letter was filled with "menaces and threats."

It became clear to Mason that Michigan would need some muscle when, on February 23, 1835, the Ohio legislature passed an act extending the northern boundaries of Henry, Williams and Wood Counties to the Harris line and marked the line with survey benchmarks.

In addition, the Ohio townships of Port Lawrence and Sylvania were created. It was directed that an election would be held on the first Monday in April to vote in township officials. (Michigan had also called the township it created in the Toledo Strip "Port Lawrence Township.")

CRAZY EVENTS OF APRIL 1835 CULMINATE IN THE BATTLE OF PHILLIPS CORNER

April 1 proved to be no joke in 1835 but rather the beginning of a month of strange events, as Michigan held elections for township officials in the Toledo Strip area.

On March 31, 1835, Governor Lucas had personally accompanied the latest group of Ohio surveyors to Perrysburg and arrived on April 2. When the governor was close, they sent out a delegation to accompany him, as a tongue-in-cheek written account related, "through two or three of the last miles of mud into town."

In town, a welcome was prepared for the governor, even though they weren't sure what the governor looked like. Many strangers coming into town were mistaken for him and were surprised to see people lining the streets and cheering for them, as well as ringing bells and shooting off cannons. Lucas finally arrived and reportedly (by Ohio sources) raised a volunteer militia of over six hundred men.

On April 4, Michigan held elections to select delegates for the state convention. This made Ohio mad once again, and so, on April 6, that state held elections in the Toledo Strip, an area that every few days in April 1835 seemed to have a survey or an election being conducted by one political entity or another. The Ohio legislature and Governor Lucas set up the Toledo area as an Ohio county named after him and appointed a sheriff and judge (Toledo today is still in Lucas County). It was determined that the First Court of the Common Pleas would commence in Toledo, the new county seat, on September 7, 1835.

This was the impetus that Michigan needed to enforce the new Pains and Penalties Act. Michigan governor Mason started gathering a 250-man militia. In response, the Ohio legislature voted to approve a $300,000 military budget; in response to Ohio, the territorial legislature of Michigan approved $315,000.

It was time for some action designed to resolve the obstacles in the way of Michigan statehood. Elections were held selecting congressional representatives from Michigan. Mason now believed that Michigan should be considered a state regardless of the border dispute outcome. In spite of the fact that it did not yet have electoral votes, President Jackson was sympathetic to the Michigan cause and sent Benjamin Howard of Baltimore, former congressman from Maryland, and Richard Rush of Philadelphia, former minister to Great Britain, to negotiate a settlement with Ohio and Michigan that provided for disarmament of the Great Lakes region. They wanted to foster agreement between Michigan and Ohio for another survey and for the people of the area to democratically decide if they wanted to be part of Michigan or Ohio. They arrived on April 3 and had their work cut out for them.

Once Ohio held elections in the disputed area on April 6, Michigan declared it would start enforcing the Pains and Penalties Act.

On April 7, Rush and Howard, the two negotiators, gave their report to President Jackson; they said that Ohio should finish rerunning the Harris line, and the residents in each area should vote to decide whether they wanted to be part of Michigan or Ohio. The winner would govern the area until Congress could rule on the issue.

On April 10, Benjamin Howard wrote to President Jackson about the situation and stated that there were "men galloping about, guns getting ready, wagons being filled with people and hurrying off, and everybody in commotion." This was because, two days before, on April 8, Michigan's Monroe County sheriff Nathan Hubble and a posse went into Toledo and began arresting violators of the Pains and Penalties Act. One of the more well-known of these incidents involved two guests of Major Stickney, Dr. Nadam Goodsell and George McKay. After breaking down the door, the Monroe sheriff's posse entered Major Stickney's house in the dead of night. While being threatened with

bodily harm by Goodsell, Hubble had to wrestle a gun from McKay. Indiana Stickney and Mrs. McKay escaped from the house and went toward town screaming for help. The Monroe posse held the prisoners for two days and then held a mock trial and released them on bail.

In seeming acceptance of the Howard and Rush agreement, Lucas pulled the Ohio militia out of Toledo. Mason did not approve of the agreement, calling it "dishonorable and disreputable." Newspaper accounts reported that "two or three hundred" Michigan horsemen came into Toledo on April 8, when, finding the Ohio electors and militia had fled, they stayed in the city for a few days and caused general havoc and mischief. This included tying an Ohio flag to the tail of a horse, a flag a Michigan newspaper called "the disgraceful badge of treason." Incidentally, Ohio is the only state whose flag could more properly be called a banner than a flag.

Because of the arrests of April 8, the Ohio officials of Toledo elected on April 6 made a hasty exit from the area. It was reported that the man elected justice of the peace "fled to the woods, where he lived many days in an old sugar shanty. It was currently reported, and generally believed among the Ohio partisans, that a miracle had been wrought on his behalf—that "robin red-breasts" brought him his daily food and drink. The belief in this "miracle" was said to inspire Ohioans engaged in the conflict.

Governor Lucas sent a new party out to once more measure the borderline. On April 20, he received word from the surveying party that they were out of supplies, the land was impassable and they had heard that General Brown was organizing a Michigan militia to come and find them.

Ohio rerunning the same Harris line did not sit well with Michigan governor Mason. On April 25, he wrote to Lewis Cass, now secretary of war in Jackson's cabinet, appealing for federal intervention. On April 29, he told Jackson's secretary of state that if the Ohio militia crossed the Fulton line, Michigan would resist them.

What Mason didn't mention was that the Battle of Phillips Corner had been waged on April 25, three days earlier. Governor Lucas, intending to rerun the Harris line, had forty armed men guarding the surveying party. On Saturday, April 25, 1835, the Ohio surveying party—including Colonel Sebried Dodge, who was with the Ohio Corps of Engineers and surveyor and engineer for the Pennsylvania & Ohio Canal Company; Uri Seely; Jonathon Taylor; and John Patterson, along with their guards—ran its line to Phillips Corners. This was a small field fourteen miles south of Adrian, Michigan, the property of Colonel Eli Phillips of the Michigan militia (now in Seward, Ohio). Aware of the arrests already made by Michigan in the Toledo Strip, Colonel Dodge wrote to Samuel Forrer, one of the Ohio canal commissioners, "We shall start tomorrow for the northwestern corner of this state and the next time you hear from me I shall probably inform you that I am at Monroe, Michigan in jail."

The surveying party and guards decided to camp for the evening. Governor Mason told the Monroe sheriff and his

posse to be on hand if the surveying camp was spotted. They were spotted by a spy sent by William McNair, the undersheriff of nearby Lenawee County. Earlier that day, McNair had mustered thirty armed Adrian citizens to help in the coming struggle (he asked for twenty volunteers and got thirty). At about noon on Sunday, April 26, the Michiganders moved in on the less-than-happy campers. Upon going to arrest the men, one of the Michiganders proclaimed, "By virtue of the posse of Wolverines present here we will arrest you."

Ohioans invented the term "Wolverines" during the Toledo War to insult Michiganders by comparing them to what they considered a "vicious, smelly, ugly north woods animal." While Ohioans used the term to degrade people from Michigan by comparing them to a disgusting, tenacious creature, the Michiganders embraced the nickname because they liked that the wolverine was ornery, strong and unafraid. And they also liked that Ohioans hated wolverines. Ohioans not liking wolverines was enough for the University of Michigan to use it as the name for its sports teams.

On the other hand, the Ohio troops called themselves the Buckeyes, named for a tree that is not widely used by man "except occasionally as a cultivated landscape plant and sometimes for its seeds, which are carried as good luck charms." Presumably, the people who carry the seeds for good luck are from Ohio. Perhaps Michiganders liked calling the people from Ohio Buckeyes because the tree has wood that does not burn well, the bark has an unpleasant odor and the bitter nut meat is mildly toxic.

Instead of waging battle, the Ohio contingent made a run for the border, with the Michiganders shooting over their heads. They fled past the undisputed Ohio border and made it to Perrysburg by the next morning. The Battle of Phillips Corner "survivors" told tales of bloodshed and slaughter at the hands of their Michigan enemies. They stated that they had been attacked by an overwhelming force of Michigan militia and reported that while performing valiant deeds, they had been fired upon. They were forced to retreat, while their less fortunate comrades were assuredly all either killed or taken prisoner. They formally reported

these assertions to Governor Lucas, who in turn reported them to President Jackson. The Ohio militia was certain that the rest of their comrades had been massacred by the crazy Michigan posse. They ran through the swamp and brambles and lost many items of clothing, including hats, coats and trousers due to the prickly ash and blackberry bushes. In fact, most of the men who had run through the brambles came out of the woods with hardly a stitch of clothing left at all.

Meanwhile, nine of the Ohioans had taken shelter in a log cabin on the property. This group consisted of many officers: one captain, one major and three colonels. They were quickly surrounded by the Michigan volunteers and surrendered without a fight. Some Ohio accounts say that a mule in the barn got in the way of the line of fire and was the first war casualty. But as soon as they were lined up to be marched to jail, the leader made a dash for the woods. The other men followed, with the Michigan contingent firing over their heads with their rifles and muskets. Recapturing all nine, they took the prisoners to the Tecumseh jail, where six posted bail, two were released and one was retained for refusing bail. Colonel Jonathan E. Fletcher, the Ohioan who was retained because he didn't recognize the right of Michigan to demand bail, would steal the jail keys, let himself out and go riding horses with the sheriff's daughters. This caused the deputies to spend most of their time looking for him.

President Jackson asked Mason for Michigan's side of the story and was informed by Sheriff McNair that Ohio's account was greatly exaggerated, and he gave the "real facts." He said that it was a civil force that made the arrests, not an army or militia; that there was no bloodshed connected with the affair; and that nine persons in all were arrested on a civil warrant, issued by a justice of the peace. The sheriff concluded his report by stating, "The commissioners made very good time on foot through the Cottonwood Swamp, and arrived safe at Perrysburg the next morning, with nothing more serious than the loss of hats, coats, and trousers." Surveying work stopped on the borderline.

The site of the Battle of Phillips Corner is in Seward, Ohio. Prior to 2001 and before the State of Ohio's recognition of the Battle of Philips Corners with a plaque, historian Naomi Twining had erected her own plaque commemorating the battle. When she asked the State of Michigan for help to erect a sign, she said that she was "turned down flat." She figures "they're still mad."

Mustering Up the Troops or Forming a Posse?

Captain Scott of Perrysburg, Ohio, wanted to drum up some support and recruits to form a company of men to fight in the Toledo War skirmish. He enlisted one of the largest men in town, Ben Odle, who was commonly known as the "Big Odle."

The Big Odle wore a large white felt hat with a ribbon on it that read, "Recruiting for the War." As a fashion accessory, he wore a green rifleman's jacket with black lace trim. His trousers were also trimmed in black lace. He carried a big drum and incessantly beat on it for hours, walking up and down Front Street, the main street of Perrysburg, accompanied by a man carrying an American flag.

The Big Odle at first had little luck in mustering any support. And on top of that, he was disrupting the court of Judge David Higgins (one of the structures on Front Street was the Court of Common Pleas of Wood County). Judge Higgins sent the sheriff to stop the Big Odle from

beating the drum or to at least move to another area out of earshot of the court building. But the Big Odle refused to stop, citing Captain Scott as a higher authority than Judge Higgins.

When informed about the Big Odle's refusal, Judge Higgins was enraged and ordered the sheriff to arrest the Big Odle, the flag carrier *and* Captain Scott. They were quickly arrested and without delay brought before the court. After a brief exchange, the judge ordered them all sent to jail.

However, on the way to the jail, Captain Scott cited the example of General Andrew Jackson having Judge Dominik Hall arrested in New Orleans after calling for martial law. Scott declared that this precedent showed that he had higher authority than the local constabulary. Captain Scott then informed the sheriff that if the arrest continued, he would be forced to call for martial law. A crowd gathered to watch the proceedings as the sheriff let his prisoners go and then went to inform the judge of the latest complications.

After Judge Higgins heard the latest from the sheriff, he cooled down a bit from his initial rage and asked if the sheriff could at least honor the judge's original request that the drumming be confined to an area away from the courthouse. But at this point, there was no longer any need for the parading and drumming because Captain Scott had been able to recruit enough Ohio volunteers from the crowd that had gathered. The volunteers admired Captain Scott for talking himself out of being jailed, and they wanted to join him by enlisting. So the Big Odle and the flag bearer were not needed for any further recruiting duties.

MICHIGAN V. OHIO: TWO ARMIES LOST IN THE BLACK SWAMP

Volunteers, armed with pitchforks, clubs, sticks, aging pistols and any other weapon they could devise, gathered for the battles they imagined would be coming in the undeclared Toledo War.

As volunteers came forth in Perrysburg, one wealthy gentleman polished his officer's uniform, mounted his steed and set forth for the center of town, where he spied a motley crew of volunteers coming from the south. Using his officer leadership skills, he shouted them into line and started marching them toward the river—all the while hoping everyone would see him gloriously leading his troops to battle. However, it turned out that once the troops began conversing with one another, they found that no one knew of any authority the self-appointed leader supposedly had to lead them. Imagine the gentleman's surprise when he turned around and saw that everyone's muskets were pointed at him! As they questioned him about seeing proof of his commission, or any other official paperwork, they continued toward the river. The officer eventually sat on his half-drowned horse in the middle of the river, blue with cold, for a few hours until friends came and vouched for him. They allowed him to go back to the safety of his domicile, where he put away his uniform—his troop-leading days over.

The Great Black Swamp was located to the south of Toledo. It seemed to Michigan that the swamp was a natural border between Toledo and Ohio, another reason for Michigan to retain the Toledo Strip. Both the Ohio and Michigan armies entered the Great Black Swamp to engage in battle. However, both armies got lost in the almost impassable forests, wetlands and grasslands of the swamp. In the Great Black Swamp, the sky would turn black from all the invading insects, and a bite from one of the mosquitoes could give one ague or malarial fever.

Neither army was able to find the other army, so the closest they got to a battle was yelling taunts at each other across the Maumee River. After both armies slogged along in the swampy wilderness for about a week looking for an army to fight, they both got tired and went back home to tend their farms.

This inspired one newspaper to comment, "When it comes to waging a safe war, Michigan and Ohio have all the secrets: 1) Only send one army afield at a time; 2) Don't let them find each other; and 3) Make sure guns aren't used." (Most men of the two armies were armed only with sticks or clubs.)

On June 8, 1935, the Ohio legislature met and passed the Abduction Act, designed to "prevent the forcible abduction of the citizens of Ohio." This was in retaliation to the Michigan Pains and Penalties Act but did not stem the epidemic of "kidnapping" Ohio citizens in the Toledo Strip area, as arrests in the area still occurred. The Jackson negotiators took this opportunity to go back to Washington, D.C., to see if there were any further instructions. There weren't.

STICKNEY STICKS DEPUTY SHERIFF WOOD

On July 12, 1835, the deputy sheriff of Monroe County, Joseph Wood, was assigned to arrest Two Stickney for resisting two Michigan officers by force. Some accounts said that Two was defending his brother, One, from being arrested during the incident. A more probable reason given is that Two Stickney and J. Baron Davis broke up a sheriff's auction that Monroe County was holding when an Ohio sympathizer couldn't pay his debts. Davis and Stickney were identified as part of a rowdy audience that knocked down the constable and drove the horses that were being auctioned off into the woods. They then stormed the auction building and liberated the furniture that was going to be auctioned.

Warrants were issued for Two Stickney and J. Baron Davis. Two Stickney warned Deputy Joseph Wood that if he set foot in Toledo, his life would be in danger. On July 15, the sheriff heard that Davis and Stickney were at J. Baron Davis's inn, the Mansion House on Summit Street in the Toledo Strip, which was considered a "hotbed of Ohio partisans." With Constable Lyman Hurd as backup, Sheriff Wood entered the inn and saw J. Baron Davis, Two Stickney and George McKay, who was also wanted, sitting at a table playing cards. When the sheriff moved in for the arrest, McKay picked up his chair and threatened the sheriff with it. Hurd told the sheriff that unless he desisted, he would "split him down." With the rest of the tavern patrons looking on, Sheriff Wood then attempted to arrest Two Stickney. He put his hands on Stickney's shoulders and grabbed him by the collar. Two took out a small knife with a short blade called a "dirk" and stabbed Wood between the second and third ribs on Wood's left side. A dirk knife has a smaller blade than a jackknife. As he stabbed Wood, Two said those immortal words: "There, damn you, you have got it now."

Stickney, McKay and Davis made a beeline for the door and the Fulton borderline. They were not pursued, as Sheriff Wood was sure he was dying and was carried down the street to Ira Smith's Eagle Tavern. Local doctor Jacob Clark pronounced Sheriff Wood "mortally wounded"

because of his weak pulse. He dressed the wound and gave Wood some liberal doses of whiskey. Wood was sure he was mortally wounded, but after more whiskey pain medicine, he sought out a second opinion from a Dr. Southworth, since he wanted a "non-Ohio" doctor to look at it. Dr. Southworth disagreed with the previous prognosis and told Wood that he would be fine in the morning except for a bad hangover. Wood suffered the only (human) injury of the war.

When Michigan governor Mason heard of these developments, he sent two hundred Michigan militia members into Toledo to arrest Two Stickney. When the Ohioans spotted the army, they quickly fled across the Maumee River any way they could—some even paddling their way to the other side on logs or anything else that would float. Once the Ohioans were safely on the other side, only then did the Michiganders proceed to shoot their guns across the river. In true Toledo War style, no one was hurt.

The Michigan militia, chagrined that Two Stickney had gotten away, arrested more Ohio sympathizers, including, once again, Major Stickney and his friend George McKay. Major Stickney strenuously resisted, with his family attempting to intercede. It took two men to hold him on a horse for the trip to Monroe. He fell off repeatedly due to his struggles, and they finally had to tie his feet under the horse's body.

On July 18, Michigan governor Mason asked Ohio governor Lucas to extradite Two Stickney.

Governor Lucas refused the request, stating that the incident happened in Toledo, which was Ohio's territory. This did not ease tensions between the two opponents. Washington officials were starting to get upset.

A militia of about 250 men entered Toledo and arrested 6 men on civil warrants. Some of the gathering smashed down the door to the *Toledo Gazette*, a newspaper run by Ohio sympathizer Andrew Palmer, which had described the Michigan militia as "composed of the lowest and most miserable dregs of the community" and then went on to call the soldiers "low drunken frequenters of grog shops, who had been hired at a dollar a day." The *Toledo Gazette* was accused by the *Democratic Free Press* of being "the chief instigator of resistance to Michigan laws." The Michiganders vandalized the office, destroying the printing press and throwing individual pieces of typeset all around. The *Toledo Gazette* called these actions "worse than Algerian robbery or Turkish persecution." The fine art of insults has definitely changed since then.

On July 22, President Jackson's new secretary of state, John Forsyth, sent a letter to Lewis Cass stating that submitting the controversy to the federal legislature would just be "the cause for more trouble." Maybe he was peeved because he became secretary of state too late to have a Michigan county named for him, but he expressed the thought that the governors should be able to work it out for themselves. He also said that he had heard from David Disney—a delegate Governor Lucas sent to Washington to try to work things out—that Lucas wanted to abide by President Jackson's wishes and stay out of the Toledo Strip area until the issue could be debated in Congress. David Disney might as well have been Walt Disney due to the fantasy expressed in this remark. It wasn't too long after, on August 3, that General Brown told Governor Mason that Lucas was raising an army "of some magnitude" in Toledo. This was because Lucas still planned to hold court proceedings in the disputed territory on September 7 in order to strengthen Ohio's claim to the Toledo Strip. The army was to be for protection.

MASON IS FIRED! LITTLE JACK HORNER PELTED WITH PLUMS!

President Jackson let it be known that he wanted the line to be rerun and activities over the Pains and Penalties Act to stop until Congress had a chance to rule on the Toledo Strip issue.

Secretary of State Forsyth informed Cass on August 16 that President Jackson had threatened to remove Mason from office unless he followed Jackson's wishes and avoided further violence. When on August 24 Mason learned that he would be the nominee of the Michigan Democratic Party under the new state constitution, he took this as a mandate. In response to the notification of General Brown that Lucas was again raising an army, on August 25 (the day after he was nominated), Mason ordered up the volunteers and Michigan militia, expressing the desire to get two hundred troops to oppose Lucas. He also continued to prosecute people for violating the Pains and Penalties Act. Fanning the fire, a Michigan newspaper welcomed Ohioans to enter the Toledo Strip and find "hospitable graves" there.

This news made it to Washington, and on August 29, President Jackson wrote the letter removing Stevens Mason as acting governor of the Michigan Territory for continuing to arrest Ohioans in the Toledo Strip and for raising another militia. To replace Mason, Jackson tried to appoint Judge Charles Shaler of Pennsylvania. Judge Shaler proved himself to be perhaps one of the wisest men in the Toledo War incident by totally refusing the assignment.

Jackson's next choice was John S. Horner of Virginia. Of course, with a name like John Horner, and especially if you are short, you are going to get the nickname "Little Jack."

An old expression defines a politically desired position, assignment or reward as a "political plum." But this Little Jack Horner put his thumb in the pie and pulled out anything but a political plum when he accepted the territorial governorship of the Michigan Territory. The Michigan Territory was outraged that Mason had been fired by President Jackson and was more than happy to take it out on Horner. With a pompous attitude and a sour expression on his face, upon arriving in Michigan from his native Virginia, the newly appointed territorial governor immediately went to Mason's vacated office in the territorial Capitol Building and announced his presence. He thought none of the staff had heard him, so he again announced himself, a little louder, saying he was there representing the federal government, had a letter of appointment and was taking command—and still no one paid the slightest attention to him. Workers were rearranging the office, getting it ready for statehood, and just elbowed Horner out of the way while otherwise ignoring him. That night, Mrs. Horner accompanied him to a banquet at American Hall. When Mrs. Horner was introduced, she was applauded. When Governor Horner was introduced, he was loudly booed.

Horner next went to the Detroit City Hall to address a meeting of leading citizens. While he was there, he requested some legislation to be passed, but the council produced only one piece of business—a resolution asking Jackson to recall Horner back to Virginia!

When Horner announced that he would free the prisoners arrested under the Pains and Penalties Act, the newspapers accused him of being a Lucas tool and attempting to undo Mason's work. A riot was starting to assemble at the Monroe County courthouse. Horner thought he could talk to the crowd and win it over to his way of thinking. So getting on his horse, he rode to Monroe.

As he tried to speak while standing on the Monroe County courthouse stairs, the mob yelled, booed and threw clods of dirt at him. The attorney general of Monroe, James Adams, told Horner he could not do anything or they would throw both of them in the river. He warned Horner to stop talking, get on his horse and race out of there, as he thought he detected the scent of tar and feathers. Adams then announced he was quitting, and when Horner said he would not accept his resignation, Adams told him what he could do with the job. Soon, Horner announced he was going to free the prisoners, and the mob moved closer. Horner barely had time to mount his horse and make a run for it while the crowd shouted and ran after him, promising a welcoming committee with a rail for him to ride on if he ever came back. Running someone out of town on a rail was a punishment in colonial times in which a man was made to straddle a fence rail held on the shoulders of at least two men, with other men on either side to hold him upright. The unfortunate victim was then paraded through town and usually dumped at the town limits. This punishment was not only embarrassing but also extremely painful. Tarring and feathering was another punishment in earlier times in which the victim was covered with tar and then feathers.

Horner galloped along the road and didn't stop until he got to Ypsilanti, where he found an inn and hunkered down for the night. However, in the dead of night, news of what happened at the Monroe courthouse filtered into the Ypsilanti area. When it was discovered where Horner was, a noisy crowd gathered outside the inn and began throwing rocks and loudly inquiring where a rail could be found. Unsuccessful at finding a rail, the rock throwing escalated to vegetables and horse dung. In the morning, the landlady

billed Horner for the damage to the inn. Other incidents included Horner getting pelted with vegetables and being burned in effigy in Detroit.

Finally, when Horner was hiding out at another inn in Ypsilanti, Stevens Mason found him and informed him that the Wisconsin Territory was being organized and that he should go there because he would automatically be governor since the Wisconsin Territory was what remained of the Michigan Territory after Michigan became a state. Horner escaped to Wisconsin, an area much more hospitable to him—although after the reception he received in Michigan, a gulag in Siberia would have been more hospitable. He became one of Wisconsin's founding fathers and organized the city of Ripon, Wisconsin.

TOP HAT FILING SYSTEM

Events had reached such a frenzy that on August 26, 1835, the *Detroit Free Press* ran the headline: "War! War!" The newspaper went on to say, "Orders have been issued for volunteers to rendezvous at Mulhollen's in the County of Monroe, on the First of September next, for the purpose of resisting the military encroachments of Ohio." Mulhollen's was a farm on the outskirts of Monroe.

Mason, not having received the news that he was no longer acting governor of the Michigan Territory, led the Michigan militia—an ill-equipped (most still had just sticks and broom handles for weapons) but exuberant 250- to 1,000-man army (depending on which account you read) to Toledo. The goal was to prevent any Ohio judges from holding court the following day. The Ohio legislature had set September 7, 1835, as the day for the first meeting of the court, and the Michigan militia was determined that it not take place. It was, in effect, Ohio challenging Michigan to stop the court session. It took the Michigan militia four days to march to Toledo, foraging all the way. "Foraging" was basically stealing vegetables, chickens and other food from local farms. This was in spite of the fact that many Michigan farmers were happy to help feed and supply their fighting boys. One prime example of the foraging was the

group of men who raided a farmer's honey hive, ate too much honey, got deathly ill and were last seen hunched over a farmer's fence returning the honey, almost becoming the only human fatalities of the war.

The trek to Toledo by the Michigan militia recruits, many of whom were horseless and on foot, was like a pilgrimage for the soldiers because they were a new generation that had never seen any military action. The last action in the area had been the Battle of the River Raisin in 1812, twenty-three years before most of the men were born. The foraging became legendary, at least to those involved. Mock court-martial proceedings were held on the way for the theft of the many chickens, pigs and vegetables stolen from the local farmers along the way. The courts-martial were comically dismissed for "lack of evidence." Although the Toledo War was never one that one would see engraved on a soldier's tombstone like the veterans of other wars, it was an important rite of passage for many of the soldiers involved. If there had been just *one* notable battle, there might have even been Daughters of the Toledo War branches all over Michigan.

On Sunday, September 6, 1835, the majority of the troops reached Mulhollen's, about eight miles from Toledo, and pitched camp. They were expectantly hoping to meet the Ohio forces in open warfare soon, to prevent Lucas from holding court proceedings in the Toledo Strip. One inconsistency all through the Toledo War involves the records of the number of men actually involved. Michigan military records show that about 1,160 men were conscripted to fight for Michigan. This is also the only war known in which officers outnumbered enlisted men on the Michigan side. Numbers given in newspaper reports are often fanciful, such as when it was reported that the Ohio militia numbered over 10,000 men—until dismissed by Governor Lucas in accordance with the Rush-Howard agreement.

While foraging and singing, with rumors of alcohol being involved, the erstwhile soldiers made it to Toledo and made camp. Since the average time of travel was four days, the Michigan militia members were prepared to wait for the Ohio militia to show up from their rumored encampment in Perrysburg, Ohio.

Poetry being a much-appreciated art in the early 1800s, some of the militia members composed a poem for the Toledo War:

> *THE NEW COCK ROBIN*
> *"And who would cut up Michigan?"*
> *"I," says Governor Lucas*
> *"What I undertook is*
> *to cut up little Michigan."*
>
> *"And who has bid him do it?"*
> *A million freemen*
> *(Counting women and children)*
> *"'Tis Ohio bids him do it."*

"And who rings the bells of war?"
"I," says Gen'l Bell"
"'Tis I that rings the bell
Ding, dong goes my bell of war."
"And what is all this bother for?"
For Port Lawrence? No.
For Vistula? Not so.
Both died of ague last year.

But out of their graves there did spring
A little mushroom
Of sickliest bloom
Which botanists call Toledo.
The flower is Ohio's no doubt,
"'Tis Buckeye in breed
She scattered the seed:
Then let Gov. Lucas transplant it.

But the swamp where it grew is not here.
Then let him beware
How he runs up a fence there,
He will find other stings than mosquitoes.

Lucas, in the meantime, in his plan to establish jurisdiction in the Toledo area by holding court there, had judges, court officials and twenty armed guards leave Maumee, Ohio, at one o'clock in the morning on September 7. At three o'clock in the morning, they reached their destination, an old schoolhouse in the Toledo Strip area with blacked-out windows.

The Michigan militia continued to grow, and soon it was reputed by some accounts to be over ten thousand, compared to Ohio's one hundred. Upon hearing this, the Ohio judges that were supposed to have court were "confounded with fear." But the Ohio commander, Colonel Mathias Vanfleet, and company were afraid they would be laughed at if they backed out. The fearful judges were told by Colonel Vanfleet that "if you are *women*, go home. If you are men, do your duty as Judges of the Court!" They finally made for Toledo with Vanfleet's armed escort. Hastily conducting court at three o'clock in the morning in the abandoned schoolhouse (it lasted only ten minutes), they wrote the proceedings on small, loose pieces of paper that Dr. Horatio Conant stored in that very reliable filing system of the nineteenth century—the bands of his high bell crown hat.

When they finished, they woke up tavern keeper Munson H. Daniels so they could celebrate before heading back across the Fulton line. While the group was still at the bar, a prankster came into the bar and yelled that the militia was coming. In the style of previous Ohio-Michigan confrontations, the startled associate judges, who included the alliterative Baxter Bowman, Jonathan Jerome and William Wilson, took off on their horses until they discovered that there was no militia after them. In

the excitement, Dr. Conant lost his hat with the court minutes in it, having it knocked off by a low-lying tree branch while he was fleeing the phantom militia.

Because the minutes were necessary to establish that the court session had legally taken place, Conant and two other Ohio men went back on foot to search for the hat and found it as the sun was rising. They made it back past the Fulton line just after dawn—and just in time to hit the bar to again celebrate the victory. The exhilarated, alcohol-fueled party also fired a victory two-shot volley into the air.

VEGETABLES AND PIGS BEWARE—THE WEEKEND OCCUPATION OF TOLEDO

As the day dawned, the Michigan army led by Governor Mason marched into Toledo. They were not familiar with Ohio court customs of meeting at three o'clock in the morning and were confused when they found the whole area devoid of Ohio troops.

In the part of the war sometimes dubbed the "Onion Plot," the Michigan troops had fully expected to find the Ohio troops there and finally engage in an actual battle. Instead, they found the town's streets empty, with no sign of the Ohio regiment. As Charles Brown's history states, Mason himself led the troops, overrunning all the watermelon patches in his route, laying waste to the orchards and personally demolishing Major Stickney's icehouse. He then burst through Stickney's front door to capture him and carry him off as a prisoner of war to Monroe. However, only Charles Brown's account credits Mason with personally laying waste to the Stickney farm.

So the Michigan troops caroused, drank and generally partied for three days in Toledo while waiting for the Ohio troops to show up, not realizing Ohio had held its court proceedings and was finished at three o'clock in the morning, not counting the time the officials spent searching for the court notes.

Besides Major Stickney, his son-in-law Platt Card (married to Indiana) was targeted. When Michigan

troops heard suspicious noises coming from his barn, they gave warning yells first and then fired their weapons. When the smoke cleared, they found the only confirmed casualty of the war: an old mare belonging to Lewis E. Bailey. The reason this fatality was confirmed is that for every year thereafter, a bill would be introduced into the Michigan legislature asking for reimbursement for the horse. Finally, in 1846, fifty dollars—along with fifty dollars' interest—was paid.

Other unconfirmed casualties of the war were two pigs (at least one was roasted) and many chickens that disappeared, never to be seen again. A horse and mule were also made prisoners of war. Although the American Society for Judicial Settlement of International Disputes claimed that the total casualties were two horses, one on each side, the exact number of livestock plundered was never determined.

One last incident in the Toledo War, the little-known Battle of Mud Creek, occurred when Sheriff Wood, still mad about the stabbing, led a group of volunteers into the Toledo Strip to arrest the judge and the commissioners who had held the September 7 "night court." An alarm was raised among the Ohio sympathizers, and they chased the sheriff's posse, but to no avail. Even though a few shots were actually fired, the Michigan posse escaped with their prisoners. Unbelievably, Sheriff Wood, the only person to suffer injury in the war up to that point, was once again the only one injured, as he was shot in the arm during the confrontation.

Two Stickney never was apprehended for his crimes. Hiding in Sandusky, Ohio, he wrote to Governor Lucas and was told that Ohio would not pursue charges against Two. Two actually delivered the message himself to Sheriff Wood. Two later remarked, "Who needs a pardon when you have the governor on your side?"

The Michigan militia, in occupying Toledo, performed drills and was conducting a "dress parade" when a messenger arrived with a letter from Lewis Cass to Mason, consoling him on his being fired as governor—which was the first Mason had heard about it. Not long after, the letter from Jackson to Mason actually firing him arrived, after being carried to Detroit by newly appointed governor Jack Horner. Upon reading the news, Mason announced to the troops that he was no longer their commander in chief. General Brown then issued orders to disband the Michigan militia, sending everyone back to their farms and villages on September 10, although many still stuck around for a while. Since it was the anniversary of the Battle of Lake Erie, the troops shot off what was left of the state's ammunition in celebration while they marched home.

MASON IS REHIRED IN TIME FOR THE FROSTBITTEN CONVENTION

When Mason returned to Detroit from the Toledo occupation via the steamboat *General Brady*, he was treated with sympathy and admiration for sacrificing his political career for the good of Michigan.

Mason was then feted with a banquet, attended by many who had initially opposed the rule of the boy governor. With the increase in his popularity and prestige, Mason easily won election as governor of the soon-to-be new state, as the proposed constitution for Michigan was ratified on October 10, 1835. With the cessation of Toledo War hostilities and no one else willing to take the governor job after Horner fled to Wisconsin, and in spite of Mason's Michigan militia laying waste to Toledo, Mason was allowed to again assume the role of territorial governor (since he had already been elected governor) until Michigan could complete the state process. When Michigan became a state, Mason, at age twenty-five, became the youngest person ever to be a state governor, a record he will probably hold for a long time since most state constitutions require the governor to be at least thirty years of age.

Also elected were Lucius Lyon (a surveyor by profession, he was appointed surveyor general for Michigan, Indiana and Ohio in 1845) and John Norvell as senators and Isaac Crary as representative to Congress.

The original 1835 constitution document was lost for a number of years. Filing systems were not the best in those pre-digital days. While the Ohioans lost important court documents that were stuck in the band of a hat, the Michiganders lost the original document and then found it stuffed into a metal canister among some other junk ready to be tossed out. The document was restored and somewhat better preserved in the State Archives.

Although most territories first sought approval from Congress to become a state and *then* drew up a constitution and elected officials, Tennessee had done it a little differently by putting together its constitution and electing officials in 1796. Mason thought that Tennessee's actions were a precedent and, after doing the same, expected Michigan to become a state as of November 1, 1835. Mason thought Michigan would be welcomed by Congress as a fellow state and even had a state seal drawn up with 1835 as the admission date. The seal developed by Mason is the same one used today—with the same date, 1835, even though it wasn't until 1837 that Michigan officially became a state. Stevens had hoped that the border controversy with Ohio could be settled once Michigan was a state and therefore on equal footing with Ohio.

In fact, Michigan celebrated its 100th anniversary in 1935, not 1937, one hundred years after the date Mason felt was when Michigan should have become a state—although it did hedge its bets a bit by saying that the centenary would be celebrated from 1935 to 1937.

Indeed, the state of Vermont had originally been part of New York State, but the citizens of the area were tired of the poor governance and lack of law and order and, much to the chagrin of New York, declared themselves a separate state in 1777. They remained as the Vermont Republic until joining the United States as the fourteenth state in 1791.

So even though there was a precedent of other areas becoming states through the stealth method, when the U.S. Congress convened in December 1835, it refused to seat the three Michigan newcomers on the Senate floor and would let them only observe from special chairs in the Senate. By Michigan's action of sending representatives before Michigan was officially declared a state, Michigan was said to be the first to try to "break into the Union." One point of antagonism was that Michigan had included in the boundaries stated in its constitution the area of the Toledo Strip and also parts that the state of Indiana considered within its borders. Both Illinois and Indiana began to worry about the legality of their borders because of this and sided with Ohio against Michigan.

On June 15, 1836, President Jackson signed a bill that would allow Michigan to become a state if it gave up its claim to the Toledo Strip. In return, it would be given the other two-thirds of the Upper Peninsula (at that time, often called the Northern Peninsula). The fledgling state had already claimed the part of the Upper Peninsula that included the Mackinac and Sault Ste. Marie area. Michigan did not want the rest of the Upper Peninsula, and the *Detroit Free Press* referred to it as the region of perpetual snows. The *Detroit Free Press* also referred to the UP as the "Ultima Thule," a Greek term used to describe a distant place beyond the "borders of the known world." Some people even said that the possession of such a wasteland was a detriment to Michigan's future. The rest of the Upper Peninsula was not for joining the state of Michigan, either, and having its seat of representation so far away in the Lower Peninsula. They had plans to form a state of their own called Huron.

Michigan wasn't crazy about this Toledo compromise either. The Michigan Territory issued a resolution, rejecting the Upper Peninsula by saying it was a "sterile region on the shores of Lake Superior, destined by soil and climate to remain forever a wilderness." One politician complained, "I wonder why they didn't give us a slice of the moon? It would have been more valuable."

Later, Michigan realized the value of the Upper Peninsula. The Monroe County Historical Society erected a sign denoting what it called the "War with Happy Ending." The plaque's inscription insinuates that the happy ending of the Toledo War was that Michigan got the Upper Peninsula and the conflict was "bloodless"—that is, there were no human casualties. Sheriff Wood, who was knifed by Two Stickney and bled profusely, might take exception to the "bloodless" portion of the sign.

Michigan learned to like the Upper Peninsula—so much so that when it came time to determine the border between Wisconsin and the UP, Michigan, under William Woodbridge, who succeeded Mason as governor, wanted as much of the UP as he could get. Congress determined that the border with Wisconsin and Michigan would follow the Montreal River, as surveyed by Captain Thomas Cram. However, the Montreal branches off into two rivers. Even though state geologist Douglas Houghton and Captain Cram had surveyed the eastern portion, Woodbridge wanted the border to be the western portion, giving Michigan 360 more square miles. Wisconsin did not agree and claimed the border to be the eastern portion of the river. In its 1903 revision to its constitution, Michigan gave its border as the westerly branch of the Montreal River. It sent negotiators to Wisconsin, but Wisconsin held fast. Today, the border is commonly marked as the easterly branch, but the matter has never been officially resolved.

In January 1836, the Michigan statehood issue became locked up in the federal legislature. By March, it became obvious that the talks would continue to favor Ohio taking possession of the Toledo Strip, with Michigan getting the full Upper Peninsula. Michigan was not in favor of it, but there was also an added carrot that if it became a state, it would share in a $400,000 land surplus windfall to be given to each official state. Nothing would be given to territories. After spending so much on militias, Michigan needed the money.

For the Michiganders, 1836 was a year of waiting. The U.S. Congress, in its eternal wisdom, actually had two bills on the floor concerning Michigan's statehood. One was to accept the boundary of Michigan and Ohio so that Ohio received the Toledo Strip and Michigan would become a state, and the other one was only about giving statehood to Michigan. By the time both bills were resolved, it was already the middle of the year. Michigan was in a kind of political limbo this whole time. The *Toledo Blade* even ran a story in its first edition in December 1835 titled: "Is Michigan a State or a Territory?" So the act of June 15 was passed in 1836, after months of study and debate. Congress passed the Clayton Act, admitting Michigan to the Union and fixing the Ohio-Michigan boundary at the Harris line. The legislation came during an election year, and in deciding in Ohio's favor, Congress certainly considered Ohio's electoral vote, since Michigan remained a territory with no electoral vote.

The Judicial Committee of Congress gave the following reasons for the decision in Ohio's favor:

- No territory had a vested right to determine its own boundaries.
- The Northwest Ordinance *could* be altered, as evidenced by the borders of Indiana and Illinois.
- The ordinance line was drawn from an erroneous map.
- Congress had virtually approved the boundary in Ohio's favor when it admitted it into the Union.
- Ohio had put a great deal of money into the canal system with Toledo as the heart of the enterprise.

One reason the committee left out was that Ohio had electoral votes and Michigan didn't.

The Michigan delegation met on September 26, 1836. Surveying the line was once more done and completed in November, while everyone waited for Congress to convene in December. The survey results were the same, vindicating Michigan's rightful claim to the area. Michigan *still* wasn't ready to give in. The September convention turned down the act of June 15's congressional proposals 28 to 21. It was lamented that the fate of Michigan's statehood and its borders would be determined by the "avarice and greed of Ohio." This was referred to as the "Convention of Dissent."

The Whig Party was all for remaining steadfast and not giving in to Ohio. Its state convention was headlined "State's Rights Nominations," with the line below it: "Don't give up the land."

Mason by this time, September 1836, realized that the only way statehood would be achieved would be by Michigan accepting the compromise and taking the Upper Peninsula, since as a territory, the cards were all stacked against it. He never gave up hope that once Michigan became a state, it could approach the Supreme Court and reopen the border issue.

During the freezing December 1836, in an Ann Arbor building with poor heating, the meeting called the "Frostbitten Convention" was held. Called by the Democratic Central Committee, forty-nine delegates from each county, except Macomb and Monroe, met for one reason. This was to pass the agreement to give the Toledo Strip to Ohio and take the rest of the Upper Peninsula not already claimed by Michigan in compensation. Monroe County specifically boycotted the convention due to its reluctance to see Michigan give up the Toledo Strip area. One casualty of Ohio getting the Toledo Strip was that it created the "lost peninsula," an area in Monroe County that could now be accessed only by going through Ohio.

The delegates voted to accept Congress's terms—to give up the Toledo Strip to Ohio and take the Upper Peninsula—and therefore to become a state, pass go and collect $400,000. Ultimately, the UP has yielded at least $48 billion worth of iron ore alone. In comparison, the California gold strike of 1849 produced less than $1 billion worth of gold. The Whigs were against giving in and taking the UP—they complained that the second convention was probably illegal, which it probably was since Congress had only sanctioned one. The second one was put together by Mason and the state's Democrats. South Carolina senator John C. Calhoun said that the Frostbitten Convention was "just a mere caucus—got up by party machinery." He continued, "It was not only a party caucus, for party purpose, but a criminal meeting." He further asserted that those responsible should "be indicted, tried, and punished."

The Michigan Territory had its supporters, though. Former president John Quincy Adams, who returned to the House of Representatives after his presidential stint, commented, "Never in the course of my life have I known a controversy of which all the right so clearly lies on one side and all the power so overwhelmingly on the other." This was due to the fact that, as a territory, Michigan had no electoral votes, while Ohio, as an official state, had the votes needed by the Democrats. John Quincy Adams gave two three-hour speeches regarding the issue, saying that Michigan should be allowed to keep the Toledo Strip. Perhaps this did not help Michigan's cause. Who wants to sit and listen to not one but *two* three-hour speeches?

However, the U.S. Congress, after considerable debate, accepted the decision of the Frostbitten Convention and voted to admit Michigan as a state without the Toledo Strip but with the full Upper Peninsula, not just the section that Michigan had already claimed.

On December 27, 1837, Jackson announced to the Senate that the agreement had been reached, and on

January 6, the U.S. Senate approved Michigan as a state by a vote of twenty-five to ten. On January 25, the U.S. House voted in favor of the Clayton Act, thirty-two to forty-three, for admission, and the next day Michigan formally entered the Union as the twenty-sixth state. Just three weeks before, on January 7, 1837, Toledo had been officially incorporated as an Ohio city.

CONSOLATION PRIZE: THE UPPER PENINSULA—WORTH MILLIONS FROM MINERALS!

The approximately 450 square miles in the Toledo strip went to Ohio, and as a compromise, Congress gave Michigan the Upper Peninsula, taking about 9,000 square miles of valuable iron, copper and timberland that had been part of the Wisconsin Territory.

So although this seemed to end the Toledo War, it never ended the animosity between Ohio and Michigan. They continued to battle over the actual state line, arguing over each farm and township, until in 1915 they agreed to *another* survey. Even then, Michigan, though reaping benefits from the Upper Peninsula, never really gave up on getting the Toledo Strip back. New attempts were made in 1915, 1922, 1932 and 1945 to once more run surveys with the intent to reclaim land from Ohio. In 1966, Michigan filed suit in federal court to reclaim Toledo, but the suit was dismissed. That seemed to settle the land question once and for all, but the water question was still being argued until 1973, when the Supreme Court ruled against Michigan for a two-hundred-mile portion of Lake Erie near the mouth of the Maumee River. Both states wanted it because it was rumored to have gas or oil on the property.

The situation was different in 1973, when the U.S. Supreme Court intervened on the Turtle Island issue. In this decision, Turtle Island in Lake Erie was split between Ohio and Michigan. This island was once home to the Turtle Island Light, which was built in 1866 to replace the one built in 1831. It, in turn, was replaced in 1904 by the Toledo Harbor Lighthouse Co. Sadly, the Turtle Island Light fell into disrepair, and now only a portion remains, along with a few other abandoned structures on the island.

After the Toledo War, the strip settled into being part of the state of Ohio, although many Wolverine traces remain, including streets named Michigan Street, Detroit Street and Monroe Street, among others.

Reelected in 1837 with a margin of fewer than eight hundred votes, Democrat Mason had a Whig opponent, Charles C. Trowbridge, call him a coward and a traitor for making peace with Ohio.

The beginning of Mason's second gubernatorial term made the Toledo War look like a cakewalk. Stevens Mason did not run for reelection in 1839, mostly due to being blamed for financial difficulties of the new state. Most of Mason's problems had to do with the fact that he announced five ambitious state projects simultaneously. These included

the Clinton-Kalamazoo Canal, to connect Lake St. Clair with Lake Michigan; a canal at Sault Ste. Marie; a canal to connect the Saginaw River and Grand River; and railroad projects. The railroad projects included the construction of a line to run from Monroe across the southern counties to Lake Michigan. Other projects would have lines between Detroit and St. Joseph and one from St. Clair to Grand Haven. With funds drying up because of the Panic of 1837, a recession that affected the entire United States, Michigan was stuck with a lot of bad debt, for which Mason got blamed. Mason was also accused by his archenemy William Woodbridge of personally mishandling a $5 million loan. Woodbridge, with a seeming pathological hatred, was relentless in his pursuit of Mason.

It started with Woodbridge voicing dissent when Mason was named territorial secretary and subsequently acting governor (Woodbridge had been the territorial secretary for Lewis Cass). As the Toledo War unfurled, Woodbridge did his best to oppose Mason's every decision. When Michigan became a state, Woodbridge declared that the 1835 election in which Mason was elected state governor was not valid, since the constitution had yet to be ratified into law. He invited famed Whig orator Daniel Webster to town to stir up opposition to Mason and exaggerated the bungling of a $5 million loan as being all Mason's fault. It was said that he secured a false confession from a Mason associate claiming that Mason had taken a bribe. When Woodbridge succeeded Mason, he spent most of his speeches lamenting the fiscal crisis that he was left with by the Mason administration. Although Woodbridge vowed to fix the fiscal problems, he promptly resigned to join the confines of the Senate for six years and became Michigan's first one-term governor. After his Senate service, he retired to his farm at Michigan and Trumbull Streets in Detroit, which later became the site of Navin Field, Bennett Field, Briggs Stadium and Tiger Stadium before becoming an abandoned lot. That area of Detroit is still known as Woodbridge.

MASON'S THIRD WAR: THE PATRIOT WAR

In 1837–38, Mason had to rally his militia yet *another time*! As if the Black Hawk and Toledo Wars weren't enough, Mason now had the Patriot War pop up on the Michigan and Canadian borders.

The Patriot War was brought about by some residents of Upper Canada and U.S. citizens who had moved to Canada. These "patriots," as they called themselves, planned to detach the peninsula lying between the Michigan frontier and the Niagara frontier from Canada and attach it to the United States. Their base of operations was located in Michigan, and they were organized into secret groups known as Hunters Lodges. At that time, many Americans still felt rebellious against Great Britain and wished to annex Canada to the United States.

The points of assembly for the Hunter Lodges were Detroit (at the Eagle Tavern on Woodbridge Street), Fort Gratiot (Port Huron), that bastion of rebellion Mount Clemens and Gibraltar. Meetings were called, and secret military organizations were created. One of the "hunters" was Dr. E.A. Theller, an Irish enthusiast for anything opposed to Great Britain who committed some overt acts for which he was arrested, tried, convicted and sentenced to the Citadel of Quebec. He escaped from the Citadel and fled to Detroit.

In the early winter of 1837–38, straggling parties of armed men waited along the border for the ice to form on the Detroit River. This was the route over which they planned to enter Canada, unfurl their flag and establish a temporary government in rebellion against the British Crown. On February 24, 1838, a group of American patriots went across the ice to the aptly named Fighting Island. They were thwarted by the British, who killed fifteen and injured forty of the patriots. In protest, the patriots collected all the books written by visiting author Captain Frederick Marryat and burned them in front of his hotel. That must have really shown them!

When the patriots attempted to seize Fort Gratiot, they were foiled by a detachment of the Brady Guards. The Brady Guards, named for General Hugh Brady, were formed from a contingent of the Black Hawk War called the Detroit City Guards. Although they disbanded after the Black Hawk War in 1832, they later morphed into the Detroit Light Guard Armory. The Brady Guards confiscated the arms and ammunition of the patriots and took the captives to Detroit. `

In the later part of December 1837, the patriots used a small steamboat to again cross the Detroit River into

Canada and landed a short distance to the north of Windsor, Ontario. They marched down to the village, and in the engagement that followed—the Battle of Windsor—a number of men on both sides were killed and wounded. The remaining patriots scattered to the woods. By most estimates, there were twenty fatalities—a far cry from none, the total from the Toledo War.

A plot was then discovered to capture the U.S. Arsenal at Dearborn and take possession of the arms stored there. To thwart this action, a company of the Michigan militia was assigned guard duty at the arsenal. The excitement continued through 1838; however, the Battle of Windsor is considered the closing of the Patriot War.

THE END OF STEVENS MASON

To reiterate, Mason's second term, when he was reelected by fewer than eight hundred votes, was as tempestuous as his first, with Whig stalwart Woodbridge dogging him at every step. Too many commitments on the state's behalf to building canals and railroads kept Woodbridge and the Whigs on Mason's back all through his second term. This caused him to lose his taste for politics.

Consequently, after his second term, Mason quit politics and moved to New York State to practice law. He got married and kept his sense of humor, as he wrote to his father after his second child's birth that the child had "great proficiency in the arts of sleeping, eating, and bawling." Sadly, Mason died of tuberculosis on January 4, 1843, at the young age of age thirty-one and was buried in New York.

In 1935, the year determined by the State of Michigan and no one else to be the one-hundred-year anniversary of statehood, Mason was uprooted and reinterred in Capitol Park, on Griswold Street in Detroit, on the site where the original Capitol Building had been. Mason was buried under a statue located in the spot where his office had been.

The Capitol Building of Stevens Mason was built in 1828 and was in the early Greek Revival style with an Ionic portico and a tower that rose forty feet over the city. It was used as a public school after the state capital was moved to Lansing. Called the Union School, it was at that time the only high school in Detroit. It also served as a library until succumbing to a fire in 1893.

While governor, Mason instituted the policy of having Section 16 of every township reserved for a public school. He also provided for the University of Michigan and helped it move to Ann Arbor from Detroit, where it would have a base of operations to once again battle Ohio in the "Big Game" every year.

Even in death, Stevens Mason has continued to suffer indignities. His casket has been moved three times in different remodeling and reconfiguring of Capitol Park. In his present location, he appears to be a target for the local pigeons. They must be Whig pigeons. Superheroes have been engaged to protect the statue from further indignities.

THE HONEY WAR

Mason's opponent Robert Lucas was an Ohio and later Iowa Territory governor who couldn't steer clear of controversies. Accepting the governorship of the Iowa Territory, he immediately clashed with his predecessor, William B. Conway, who had been the acting governor. Conway wrote to President Martin Van Buren that "Lucas committed vexatious, ungraceful, petulant, ill-natured, and dogmatic interferences" with the legislature. Besides once again personally naming a county after himself in Iowa, as he had done earlier in the Toledo Strip, he was involved in another border skirmish, this time between Iowa and Missouri, dubbed the Honey War.

The border war was over a more than nine-and-a-half-mile strip running the entire length of the Iowa-Missouri border. It was unclear where the border was in this case, due to a number of reasons, including (surprise!) the surveying of the Louisiana Purchase.

Both sides faced each other across the border, although no injuries were reported. However, a Missouri sheriff trying to collect taxes in Iowa was put in jail, and so, to collect the tax money, upon being released he cut down three trees containing beehives and took the honey, providing the basis for the moniker Honey War. One lady, upon being told her farm was now in Iowa instead of Missouri, remarked that she was glad since she heard the soil was better in Iowa!

The First and Second Battles of Manton— for the County Seat!

In 1871, three different towns in Michigan conspired to be the Wexford County seat. It is not usually considered all that prestigious to be a county seat, at least not enough to get into a skirmish over the issue. Apparently, Wexford County was an exception to this rule, as three competing places—Sherman, Cadillac and Manton—all wanted to be the county seat.

Wexford County was established in 1840 by the Michigan territorial legislation as *Kautawabet*, a Potawami Indian phrase meaning "broken tooth." Not thrilled with the name, the county was renamed Wexford, after a region in Ireland. The first county seat was in Sherman, in the northwest corner of the county. After a few years, the matter of the county seat became a rivalry among Sherman, Manton and Cadillac.

Cadillac had wanted to be the county seat ever since it was called Clam Lake in 1876. However, Cadillac was known as a "wild frontier town." The *Detroit Post* called it "the wickedest town in the Midwest." It was even rumored that the mayor of Cadillac had advocated for the legalization of prostitution.

Even though it was growing due to the railroad, Cadillac didn't have the political power (and too bad of a reputation) in 1915 to get the county seat issue on the ballot. This caused it to form an alliance with Manton, promising to support it if Manton would oppose

Sherman—and Manton was declared the new county seat in April 1881 with a vote of 1,109 to 146. Cadillac still wanted to be the county seat, and just after Manton had received the honor, Cadillac lobbied for a county board vote to move the county seat *again*. Cadillac received the two-thirds vote necessary to put the issue on the ballot because, out of the blue, George Blue, from near Manton, voted for the new initiative. It was strongly hinted that Blue had been bribed. In a vote on April 4, 1882, almost exactly a year after Manton became the capital, Cadillac won the prize, 1,363 to 309. Manton residents were mad, feeling that Cadillac had manipulated them. Some townships even destroyed their ballots in protest.

Once Cadillac won the designation as county seat, it was ready for the next step. In the early dawn following Election Day, after celebrations involving prodigious amounts of alcohol, a train went from Cadillac to Manton. It quietly backed into town, making as silent a stop as a train can make—right in front of the courthouse. In about a half hour, most of the county records and furniture had been loaded onto the train by the sheriff and twenty "specially deputized" citizens. As they struggled to load the first of three safes onto the train, the slumbering citizens of Manton awoke. What happened next depends on which town's version you believe. The Cadillac version has over two hundred Manton residents chasing the outnumbered Cadillac contingent back onto the train. In the Manton version, the whole town was deserted except for a few brave men who

went to the courthouse and confronted the "Cadillackers." Overturning the safe, they chased the Cadillackers "back to Cadillac in fear" without any of the safes. This was the First Battle of Manton.

When the Cadillackers made it home, they recruited several hundred still-celebrating city officials, mill hands and other concerned citizens to make a run back to Manton for the three safes. The provisions included a barrel of whiskey, firearms borrowed from the local hardware store, clubs, brooms, poles and crowbars—basically the same armaments as in the Toledo War. Also traveling with the alcohol-fueled group was what every battle needs: a brass band! Thus began the Second Battle of Manton.

Highlights included the Cadillac contingent claiming that the Mantonites tried to hang the county clerk and that the Manton women tried to grease the rails with butter and lard so the train couldn't move. In the Manton version, the town was invaded by an inebriated mob of five to six hundred Cadillackers. In any case, there were no fatalities, and the only shots fired were the victory volleys by the Cadillac contingent when it finally arrived back in Cadillac with its plunder, the three safes. And Cadillac remained the county seat.

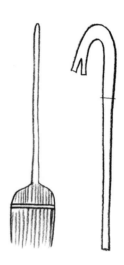

THE KING OF BEAVER ISLAND

James Jesse Strang was born in New York in 1813, and by 1836, when he was twenty-three, he had established a law practice. In 1844, he met Joseph Smith, the founder of the Mormon Church. He converted to Mormonism and was assigned by Joseph Smith to found a new branch in Burlington, Wisconsin. When Joseph Smith was killed, Strang produced a document signed by Smith that named Strang the head of the church in case anything happened to him. Not as strong in the church as Brigham Young, when Strang did not become the ultimate leader, he took his band of followers—who eventually numbered over twelve thousand—and went from

Illinois to Wisconsin. In 1848, they went to Beaver Island, in Lake Michigan, at the top of the Lower Peninsula.

After declaring he had discovered buried sacred brass plates because of a vision, Strang added two documents to the Mormon lore for his followers, the "Voree Record" and the "Book of the Law of the Lord." Another vision caused him to declare himself king of Beaver Island.

For six years, he reigned as king. About three hundred followers attended his coronation in 1850 in which he wore a bright red flannel robe, breastplate and tin crown and carried a wooden scepter.

Objecting to the Mormon lifestyle (especially polygamy), Strang was arrested and charged with treason, counterfeiting, trespassing on government land and theft by local police. He was brought to Detroit to stand trial, and the one-time lawyer defended himself well enough to earn an acquittal. At this point, he became well known enough to be elected twice to the U.S. House of Representatives, where he helped draft legislation establishing the counties of upper Lower Michigan.

As king of Beaver Island, Strang made many enemies by exerting kingly authority over islanders not in his religious sect. This caused much animosity, and members of Strang's sect were beaten when going to retrieve their mail. Hostilities intensified in the War of Whiskey Point, in which Strang's followers were attacked and Strang surprised the attackers by firing a cannon over their heads, ending the battle.

James Strang was shot by a group of four conspirators on June 16, 1856; he died three weeks later of his injuries—on July 8, designated as "King Day" by his followers. Following Strang's death at the age of forty-three, the rest of the Mormons were driven off the island by non-Mormons from Mackinac Island and thereabouts. No one was ever arrested or punished for this illegal removal. Thus ended the Kingdom of Beaver Island.

IT DOESN'T PAY TO BE LIEUTENANT GOVERNOR

In the grand tradition of vice presidents, lieutenant governors are not well remembered. Second in command for Stevens Mason's two terms, the first lieutenant governor of Michigan was Edward Mundy. He was later a judge. He was the first victim of what the newspapers called the "new Whig reign of terror."

Colonel Edward Brooks, merely upset to see a Democrat in "Whig territory," the part of the Capitol Building where the Whigs hung out, knocked down Mundy and began hitting him with a cane until he was pulled off by other people. This wasn't Mundy's only indignity. While Mason got a great statue to honor him on his grave site, the only trace of a burial spot for Edward Mundy is a tombstone for his wife that names her as the wife of the Honorable Edward Mundy. There is no trace of a memorial for Edward Mundy, although one would assume he would be buried near her since he is named on *her* tombstone. Lieutenant governors are given the sobriquet "Honorable" for life after service.

Mundy did do better in life than the second lieutenant governor, James Wright Gordon, who was also the second governor, succeeding William Woodbridge when Woodbridge was elected to the Senate. Gordon was later consulate to Brazil and died at the age of forty-four by falling from a second-floor balcony in Pernambuco, Brazil. This was mysterious since his predecessor died the same way. The only information about his burial is that it was "somewhere in Brazil." In the 1980s, a group wishing to honor former governors at their burial spots conducted a search in Brazil to find Gordon's burial place but was unsuccessful.

Thomas J. Drake, the third lieutenant governor, is not considered "famous" by the Find-A-Grave website, even though it has a long list of his accomplishments, including member of the Michigan Territorial Council, 1828–1931; member of the Michigan State Senate, Third District, 1839–41; presidential elector for Michigan, 1840; Whig candidate for U.S. representative from Michigan, Third District, 1856; delegate to the Republican National Convention from Michigan, 1856; and justice of the Utah Territorial Supreme Court, 1862–69. However, lieutenant governor of Michigan is not even mentioned. This is typical of the low regard the office holds. In fact, no one even knows where the graves for George Coe, the eleventh lieutenant governor; Edmund Fitzgerald, the twelfth; Joseph R. Williams, the fourteenth; Moreau S. Crosby, the twenty-second; Archibald Buttars, the twenty-third; Thomas Dunstan, the thirtieth; Orrin Robinson, the thirty-first; John Ross, the thirty-fourth; Allen Stebbins, the thirty-seventh; Frank Murphy (not the former governor and Supreme Court justice), the forty-second; John Connolly, the forty-third; Eugene C. Keys, the forty-fifth; Clarence Reid, the forty-eight; and Thaddeus Lesinski, the fifty-first, are located. William Vandenberg, the forty-seventh lieutenant governor, was the only one who thought the position was important enough to be mentioned on his headstone. And even then, the lieutenant governor inscription is in very small letters.

The Culmination of Years of Hostilities—the Big Game!

In 1897, the college football teams of the University of Michigan (U of M) and Ohio State University (OSU) met for the first time. The animosities of the Toledo War, even though it had been over for more than sixty years, were still fresh in the minds of the people of the once warring states.

Since there was never an actual meeting of two opposing teams in the Toledo War, the losses of their grandparents were avenged by the OSU and U of M football teams. In what became a game with no fancy name, simply the "Big Game," the two teams met for battle. Some say the Michiganders were driven by vengeance for the losses of the Toledo War, at least the Michigan portion who felt the Upper Peninsula was not a good trade for Toledo. It was a natural progression to have a football game, since many instances in the Toledo War were similar to football. Both teams had declared the other "offside," and the Michigan militia chased the Ohio soldiers past the "line of scrimmage" (the Fulton line). With Michigan winning the first football contest 34–0, the rivalry only intensified.

U of M came to dominate the Big Game, winning fifty-eight games to forty-five for Ohio State, with six ties, as of 2014. The "Big Game" has decided the Big Ten championship thirty-two times since the contest was moved in 1935 to the last Saturday in the season; on eighteen of those occasions, Michigan and Ohio State settled the title between themselves. The last game of the Big Ten season had often decided who went to the Rose Bowl, back when the Rose Bowl was always a game between the winners of the PAC-10 and Big Ten conferences.

Ironically, there has been much more bloodshed and physical damage as a result of this annual Big Ten Conference football game than there ever was in the Toledo War. This is the game touted in a survey by ESPN as the number one sports rivalry in the United States. The Michigan team was victorious in all the ensuing games until 1919, when Ohio State posted its first victory against the U of M insurgents (this was the sixteenth time they met; OSU and U of M tied in 1900 and 1910).

Although the Toledo War is not considered a "real" war by historians, and the war is not well known to most history students, the U of M–OSU game is much more well known and has national coverage, sometimes deciding the national college football championship. The cheapest ticket in the seats with the worst view of the Michigan "Big House" or Ohio State University's "Ohio Stadium" is in the neighborhood of $600.

In 1970, an Ohio judge dismissed an obscenity charge against an Ohio State student wearing a shirt that read, "F$#% Michigan" because the shirt denoted "accurate feelings" of locals about U of M and the state of Michigan.

The animosity between the two states has led the Ohio State community to follow fabled Ohio State coach Woody Haye's example and refuse to even say Michigan's name. The phrase "that state up north," abbreviated TSUN—or just "state up north," abbreviated SUN—is used instead.

In 1950, the two teams played in a blizzard with twenty-nine inches of snow, referred to as the "Snow Bowl." More than fifty thousand fans sat through the whole game. Michigan's kicker, Chuck Ortmann, punted twenty-four times, and the Wolverines *still* won 9–3, in spite of the fact that they didn't score a first down in the whole game. The Buckeyes' coach, Wes Fesler, "quit" a few days later. This was the impetus for Ohio State to hire a coach away from Miami of Ohio—Woody Hayes.

Woody Hayes was a Michigan hater through and through. Hayes was born in Clifton, Ohio, and played center on his high school team and tackle at Denison University. He became head football coach at his alma mater after stints at a couple Ohio high schools. From there, he went on to Miami University (in Ohio), where he led the team to a victory in the Salad Bowl over Arizona State University. This success led him to become the head coach at Ohio State. As head coach from 1951 to 1978, he compiled a 205-61-10 record, winning five national championships ('54, '57, '61, '68 and '70) and thirteen Big Ten Conference titles. Four Heisman Trophy winners thrived under his tutelage (including Archie Griffin, the only two-time winner in the history of the trophy).

In 1968, with Ohio State leading 48–14, Woody decided to go for a two-point conversion rather than a simple kick for an extra point. When the conversion was successful, it brought the score to a full fifty points. Asked why he "went for two," Hayes responded, "Because I couldn't go for three."

Besides the damage inflicted to Michigan on the playing field, Woody also issued punishment in an unofficial capacity—he tended to hit people a lot. In 1956, Hayes hit a television cameraman after his team lost to the University of Iowa. In 1959, Hayes tried to take a swing at *Los Angeles Examiner* sportswriter Al Bine but missed and instead hit the brother of *Pasadena Independent* sports editor Bob Shafer. Returning his fury to Michigan, in 1971, he tore up the sideline markers because of his disappointment in a missed defensive pass interference call. In 1972, he struck a Michigan State Spartan student who uttered a four-letter greeting to the coach. The last straw was when Woody struck Clemson player Charlie Bauman after Bauman intercepted a pass for the Clemson Tigers in the Gator Bowl of December 29, 1978. This was pronounced at the time (by ESPN) to be "the most unsportsmanlike play of all time." Pulitzer Prize–winning columnist Jim Murray said of Hayes, "A lot of people were surprised to hear that Woody Hayes suffered a heart attack last spring, because they didn't think he had one." Woody probably inflicted more long-range damage to Michigan than Toledo War antagonist Two Stickney and is consequently much more famous.

Also famous is Michigan head coach (and former Hayes protégé) Bo Schembechler, the butt of many Woody Hayes tirades. For ten years, the two teams dominated the Big Ten, splitting ten conference titles between them and finishing second eight times. Schembechler loved nothing more than beating his old mentor. Consequently, Schembechler was hated as much in Ohio as Hayes was in the rest of the Big Ten Conference. This was reflected in the name of an Ohio punk band calling itself the "Dead Schembechlers."

After a decade of memorable battles in the ongoing war, Michigan held a small 5-4-1 advantage. This decade is sometimes called the "Ten-Year War." Woody Hayes insisted that his team sleep in Toledo, on the "hallowed ground" of Ohio, the night before a game, not in the state of Michigan. Woody Hayes would drive sixty miles out of the way to avoid driving in Michigan, and he would refuse to buy gasoline while in Michigan even if his car was close to running out of gas. He said, "I'll tell you why we don't. It's because I don't buy one goddamn drop of gas in the state of Michigan. We'll coast and push this goddamn car to the Ohio line before I give this state a nickel of my money!"

The "Big Game" rivalry tactics were elevated to map fraud when, on the 1978–79 official State of Michigan map, the towns of Goblu ("Go Blue") and Beatosu ("Beat OSU") appeared for the first (and only) time, both located in Ohio.

Besides the annual rivalry of the Michigan–Ohio State football game, in the 1960s, another controversy over the state boundaries became a point of contention between Ohio and Michigan. Michigan said that the Clayton Act applied only to territory on land and wanted control of 206 square miles of underwater land that had been controlled by Ohio since the Toledo War. The Supreme Court ruled in 1973 that the territory would remain part of Ohio. There is still a group calling itself the Michigan militia that claims that part of Ohio really belongs to Michigan. It says that since the Harris line is now official, the northernmost two miles of Sandusky (including the amusement park Cedar Point) should be immediately returned to Michigan.

POLITICAL CORRUPTION IN DETROIT

Most of the major corruption in Michigan seems centered on the city of Detroit. An early example was Charles E. Bowles, who in 1929 ran on a law-and-order platform. This was during Prohibition, and Bowles had ties to both the Purple Gang and the Ku Klux Klan; thus, he did little to stop the gang warfare that took over the streets of Detroit. When he fired the police chief after the chief was conducting a number of raids, a successful recall election was called. He was actually removed from office after only six months.

In 1939, Mayor Richard Reading of Detroit was convicted of taking bribes from Detroit underworld mobsters. The former semipro wrestler sold protection to numbers racketeers and promotions to police officers. He was known as "Double Dip Dick" because he demanded kickbacks for his son, as well as for himself. He was convicted in 1942 and sentenced to five years in prison. Also convicted were many others in a wide-ranging scandal that began when Janet McDonald, girlfriend of a mobster, dressed her eleven-year-old daughter, Pearl, in a pink party dress before murdering her and then killing herself. The suicide note she left telling that her boyfriend was a bagman for the mob and the names she named in the note led to the most widespread corruption scandal of its day, netting, besides the Detroit mayor, 150 others, including the county prosecutor, city council members, the county sheriff and many police officers. That was probably the biggest scandal in Detroit until 2002, when Kwame Kilpatrick became mayor.

Louis Miriani was mayor of Detroit from 1957 until 1962. In 1957, he refused to greet delegates to an Islamic convention because he felt that some speakers were "anti-American," and in 1959, he refused to attend a gathering for a top Soviet official in Detroit because it was "not in the public interest." Although he made only $25,000 a year as mayor, Miriani was somehow able to acquire over $261,000, which he did not pay taxes on. Convicted of tax evasion, he spent 294 days in prison in 1970 and 1971.

THE REIGN OF KING KWAME, THE HIP-HOP MAYOR

It was the year 2001, and the city of Detroit was ready for a dynamic young mayor. Stepping up was Michigan state senator Kwame Kilpatrick, the son of U.S. representative Carolyn "Cheeks" Kilpatrick. In 1996, Kwame had won the same seat in the Michigan House of Representatives that his mother had vacated after she was elected to the U.S. House. In 2001, Kwame became the first African American to hold the Michigan house minority position.

In 2001, Kwame, at thirty-one years old, was elected the youngest mayor in the three-hundred-year history of the city of Detroit. He defeated famous city councilman Gil Hill, who appeared in the *Beverly Hills Cop* movie as himself. Called the "hip-hop" mayor, Kwame sported an earring in one ear and was very sartorial in his dress.

In his first term, Kwame was criticized for using city funds to lease a car for his family and using a city-issued credit card to buy thousands of dollars' worth of extravagant dining, expensive wines and spa massages. But this was only the tip of the iceberg.

In 2002, Kwame held an alleged party at the mayoral residence, the Manoogian Mansion. Complete with strippers, the party was supposedly interrupted by the mayor's wife, Carlita, who allegedly assaulted one of the dancers. Later, a scandal would arise over the drive-by shooting murder of this dancer.

In spite of being named on *Time* magazine's "Worst Mayors" list, Kwame was somehow elected to a second term. Starting off his second term with a bang, Kwame was removed as special administrator of the water board, a power long wielded by Detroit mayors. This was due to Kwame's going over the water board and city council's heads and awarding contracts to three different groups, one a no-bid contract he gave to a close personal friend. Soon after, the 2005–06 city audit was fourteen months late, costing the city an additional $2.4 million in penalties.

Police officers Harold Nelthrope and Gary Brown were let go by Kwame and subsequently sued, saying they were fired in retaliation for investigating abuses by Kwame and his private guard unit, the EPU (Executive Protection Unit). The two whistleblowers were awarded $8.4 million, and Kwame railed against the "wrong verdict" while blaming it on white suburbanites. Vowing to appeal the verdict, he did a quick turnaround and approved the award after hearing that text messages between the mayor and his assistant, Christie Beatty, would be made public during an appeal. A confidentiality agreement was signed, of which the Detroit City Council was unaware when it approved the $8.4 million judgment.

The terms of the confidentiality agreement came to light through the Freedom of Information Act. It wasn't long before the *Detroit Free Press* daily newspaper was printing summaries of the more than fourteen thousand text messages that Christine Beatty and Kwame Kilpatrick sent to each other on their city-owned pagers while conducting an affair.

After the spicier and most incriminating texts were released to the public, the city council voted seven to one to ask the mayor to resign. The city council had been having its own meltdowns—with U.S. representative John Conyers's wife, Monica, and fellow council member Martha Reeves of the Motown group Martha and the Vandellas, along with others, singing "Onward Christian Soldiers" in the middle of a city council meeting. Martha Reeves would lose her seat after describing her city council gig as a "second job" to her rock revival gigs, and Monica Conyers would go to jail for two years and three months for taking bribes.

Investigations revealed that Kwame had funneled state funds into two organizations—Detroit 3D and UNITE—run by his friends and wife, that wouldn't divulge what the funding was used for. Employment by the Kwame administration became known as the "friends and family plan" since so many Kwame family members were employed without experience or qualification and then given hefty raises.

Kwame ignored the city council's resolution to resign, saying it didn't have the authority to force his resignation—which caused the council to investigate other ways to remove the mayor. Petitions were circulated, and on May 14, 2008, the city council voted to request that the governor of Michigan remove Kwame from office.

Kwame was brought up on eight felony counts by Kim Worthy, Wayne County prosecutor, for perjury, misconduct in office and obstruction of justice. Later added were two more counts for assaulting or interfering with a law officer. Kwame posted bail and then took a trip to Windsor, Ontario, across the bay in Canada. He was arrested for leaving the country while out on bail and spent a night in the Wayne County jail.

Convicted on two felony counts, Kwame accepted a plea agreement to spend four months in the Wayne County jail, surrender his license to practice law, be on five years of probation and not run for public office during his probation period. He also was required to submit his resignation as mayor of Detroit.

After finally resigning as mayor and serving his four months, Kwame moved to posh furnishings in Texas with his wife and three sons. Set up on a plan to reimburse the city, Kwame was once more called back to Detroit to serve 120 additional days when he neglected to make his payments.

On June 23, 2010, Kilpatrick was revealed to have been the target of FBI and SEC investigations. He was indicted on nineteen federal counts, including ten counts of mail fraud, three counts of wire fraud, five counts of filing a false tax return and one count of tax evasion. Each count of fraud carried a maximum sentence of twenty years' imprisonment and a fine of $250,000. Each tax count carried a maximum sentence of three to five years.

Kwame Kilpatrick used a personal organization, the Kilpatrick Civic Fund, to pay for personal and election expenses. These expenses included buying golf clubs, paying for summer camp for his children, covering his family's personal travel and a lease on a Cadillac DeVille.

Also indicted were Kwame's best friend, Bobby Ferguson, and Kwame's father, Bernard Kilpatrick. During the trial, it was revealed that Kwame steered work to Ferguson for kickbacks. His father helped collect the kickbacks required by the "Kwame Corporation" to do business with the City of Detroit. All three were convicted, with Kwame convicted on twenty-four counts, including racketeering, extortion, mail fraud and tax evasion, on March 11, 2013. On October 10, 2013, he was sentenced to twenty-eight years in prison.

Bibliography

Appeal by the Convention of Michigan. Detroit, MI: Sheldon & McKnight Printers, 1835.

Badenhop, S.W. *Federal Failures: The Ohio-Michigan Boundary Dispute*. Bowling Green, OH: Graduate College of Bowling Green, 2008.

Bald, F.C. *Michigan in Four Centuries*. New York: Harper & Row Publishers, 1961.

Barnett, L., and R. Rosentreter. *Michigan's Early Military Forces*. Detroit, MI: Wayne State University Press, n.d.

Brown, Charles. *The Government of Ohio, Its History, Resources and Jurisprudence*. Kalamazoo, MI: Moore & Quale, 1875.

Burcar, C. *It Happened in Michigan: Remarkable Events That Shaped History*. Guilford, CT: Morris Book Publishing, 2010.

Catton, B. *Michigan: A History*. New York: W.W. Norton & Co., 1984.

Dickson, K.R. *Benjamin Franklin Stickney and the Maumee Valley*. Point Place, OH: ZKDATT Publishing, 2009.

Dunbar, W.F., and G.S May. *Michigan: A History of the Wolverine State*. Grand Rapids, MI: William B. Eerdsmans Publishing Co., 1995.

Emmanuel, Greg. *The 100-Yard War: Inside the 100-Year-Old Michigan-Ohio State Football Rivalry.* New York: Wiley, 2005.

Faber, D. *The Boy Governor: Stevens T. Mason and the Birth of Michigan Politics.* Ann Arbor: University of Michigan Press, 2012.

———. *The Toledo War: The First Michigan-Ohio Rivalry.* Ann Arbor: University of Michigan Press, 2008.

George, Sister Mary Karl. *Drums Along the Maumee.* Lansing: Michigan Natural Resources Magazine, 1973.

———.*The Rise and Fall of Toledo, Michigan…The Toledo War!* Lansing: Michigan Historical Commission, 1971.

Irish, B. "Seeking Michigan: Battle for Wexford County!" Seeking Michigan. 2013. http://absolutemichigan.com/category/michigan-pages/pages-history.

Judicial Settlement of International Disputes. Vol. 11. American Society for Judicial Settlement of International Disputes. 1913. [Retrieved from Google Books.]

Knapp, J.I. *Illustrated History and Biographical Record of Lenawee County, Michigan.* Ann Arbor: University of Michigan, 1935.

McNair, William. *The Battle of Phillips Corner.* Michigan Pioneer Collections, XII, 409–11. 1888.

Millard, Alfred L. *Early History of Lenawee County and of the City of Adrian.* Adrian, MI: Lenawee County Historical Society, 1876.

Mitchell, G. "History Corner: Ohio-Michigan Boundary War." *Professional Surveyor* (June/July 2004).

Nunnally, Michael L. *American Indian Wars.* Jefferson, NC: McFarland & Co., Inc., 2010.

Path, J. *The Toledo War and the Battle of Phillips Corners.* Adrian, MI: Lenawee County Historical Society, 2011.

Romig, W. *Michigan Place Names.* Detroit, MI: Wayne State University Press, 1896.

Rubenstein , B.A., and L.E. Ziewacz. *Michigan: A History of the Great Lakes State*. Wheeling, IL: Harlan Davidson Inc., 2002.

Sagendorph, K. *Stevens Thomson Mason: Misunderstood Patriot*. New York: E.P. Dutton Company, Inc., 1945.

Scribner, H. *Memoirs of Lucas County and the City of Toledo*. Madison, WI: Western Historical Association, 1910.

Sielicki, J. "Toledo War Wins Notice." *Toledo Blade*, December 1, 2013.

Stein, M. *How the States Got Their Names*. New York: Harper Collins Publishers, 2008.

Tucker, S.C. *The Encyclopedia of the War of 1812*. N.p., 2012. [Retrieved from ABC-Clio database.]

Utley, Henry M., and Byron Cutcheon. *Michigan as a Province, Territory and State*. New York: Publishing Society of Michigan, 1906.

Verhage, K. "Recalling the 'Battle of Manton.'" CadillacNews.com. 2013. http://www.cadillacnews.com/news_story/?story_id=181 0716&year=2013&issue=20130706.

Way, Willard. *The Facts and Historical Events of the Toledo War of 1835*. Toledo, MI: Daily Commercial Steam Book and Job Printing House, 1869.

ABOUT THE AUTHOR

Alan Naldrett was the founder of one of the first used vinyl student record stores while earning his bachelor's degree at Michigan State University. By the time he earned master's degrees in information science and archival science, he had been a blues and rock musician, as well as a stock and insurance broker, real estate agent and comic book store owner. He divides his time between being a librarian and an author, having written and co-written three local history books and writing a number of history articles for various publications. In "Big Game" battles, he tends to lean toward whichever team's win would help Michigan State the most.